How to Become a Boss Negotiator in Business and Life

Mastering the Art of Negotiation with Anyone, at Anytime, and Anywhere

Sam O.A

Copyright © 2023 by Sam O.A

All Rights Reserved. This document is intended to provide accurate and dependable information about the subject and issues discussed. The publication is sold with the understanding that the publisher is not obligated to provide accounting, legally permissible, or otherwise qualified services. If legal or professional advice is required, a practicing member of the profession should be contacted.

From a Declaration of Principles that was unanimously accepted and approved by an American Bar Association Committee and a Publishers and Associations Committee. No portion of this document may be reproduced, duplicated, or transmitted electronically or in printed form. The recording of this book is expressly forbidden, and storage of this content is not permitted without the publisher's written consent. All right is reserved.

The information contained herein is stated to be accurate and consistent, and any liability incurred as a result of inattention or otherwise as a result of the recipient reader's use or abuse of any policies, processes, or directions contained herein is sole and complete. Under no conditions will the publisher be held liable for any reparation, damages, or monetary loss incurred as a result of the information contained herein, either explicitly or implicitly.

All copyrights not held by the publisher are owned by the respective author(s).

The information contained herein is provided solely for informational purposes and is therefore universal. The information is presented without contract or assurance of any kind.

The trademarks are used without the trademark owner's consent, and the trademark is published without the trademark owner's permission or support. All trademarks and brands mentioned in this book are solely for clarity purposes and are owned by their respective owners, who are not affiliated with this document.

For Questions and enquiries contact; sam@samamoo.com

ISBN: 978-1-63750-387-4

SA-Publishing

Special Bonus

SPECIAL BONUS!

Want These 2 Bonus EBooks For Free?

Get FREE, Unlimited Access To These and All of Our New Books By Joining Our Community

Scan With Your Camera to Join

Other Books

- How to be More in Tune with The Feelings of Your Customers
- Time Management For Busy People
- Sell Like titans

Table of Contents

HOW TO BECOME A BOSS NEGOTIATOR IN BUSINESS AND LIFE . 1

SPECIAL BONUS 4

OTHER BOOKS 5

INTRODUCTION 8

CHAPTER 1 13

UNDERSTANDING THE ART OF NEGOTIATION 13
HOW TO IDENTIFY YOUR NEGOTIATING STYLE AND USE IT TO YOUR ADVANTAGE 22
TYPES OF NEGOTIATION STYLES 29
HOW TO SET THE RIGHT EXPECTATIONS BEFORE YOU START NEGOTIATING 36
HOW TO ASK QUESTIONS TO GATHER INFORMATION AND BUILD RAPPORT .. 43

CHAPTER 2 48

HOW TO TURN A NEGOTIATING TACTIC INTO A STRATEGIC ADVANTAGE 48
How to Get the Most out of a Negotiation 54
How to Manage Yourself During a Negotiation 57
How to Deal with People Who Don't Want to Negotiate or Just Want to "Win" 62

CHAPTER 3 67

HOW TO PREPARE FOR A NEGOTIATION 67
How to Deal with Common Negotiating Mistakes 71
How to Avoid Being Trapped in a Negotiation 75
How to Start & End a Negotiation 78

CHAPTER 4 85

THE BEST STRATEGIES TO PERSUADE OTHERS 85
How to Listen and Make Others Feel Comfortable 89
How to Win Arguments and Debates 100
The Four-step Model of an Argument 103

CHAPTER 5 108

HOW TO WORK WITH DIFFERENT PERSONALITIES AND PERSONALITY TYPES

    An Extrovert's Personality 108
    A Controller's Personality 109
    An Introvert's Personality 110
    An Empathizer's Personality 111
    A Challenger's Personality 112
    The 7 Types of People You Are Likely to Meet in a Negotiation 116
    How to Avoid Being Bullied in the Process of Negotiation 118
    Negotiating Skills for Bullies 120

CHAPTER 6 123
    HOW TO BECOME A MASTER NEGOTIATOR AND ACHIEVE SUPERIOR RESULTS 123
    Why Should You Negotiate? 123
    How to become a master negotiator 127
    The Top 10 Secrets of Masterful Negotiation 128
    How to Negotiate when You're Under Pressure 134
    The 5 Mindset Changes You Must Make to Succeed as a Negotiator 139

CHAPTER 7 145
    THE 8 MOST COMMON PITFALLS OF NEGOTIATION 145
    The 3 Most Important Questions to Ask Before Your First Negotiation 151
    What's Your Bottom Line? 154
    6 Ways to Make a Negotiation Winnable 155
    What makes a Negotiation Winnable? 157
    10 Rules to Remember When Negotiating 161

SPECIAL BONUS 167

THANK YOU! 168

ABOUT THE AUTHOR 170

O T H E R   B O O K S 171

Introduction

Learn how to negotiate like a boss, whether you're in business, selling a house, or even negotiating a salary at your job.

The art of negotiation is a critical life skill that everyone should master. This is especially true for those who are trying to negotiate a better salary, buy a home, sell their house, or start a new business. But what is the best way to negotiate? How do you negotiate effectively? What if you don't know how to negotiate?

These are common questions. But it's not always as easy as asking a question and receiving an answer.

In this book, I will show you how to negotiate like a boss in all types of situations. I'll show you how to approach people, talk to them, and get what you want without coming across as needy, desperate, or weak.

A lot of people believe that they're good negotiators, but the truth is, most people suck at it. Even if you're pretty good at the negotiation game, if you don't understand its nuances, you'll wind up wasting time, money, and resources.

This is the book I wish I had when I started my business.

It's full of real-life examples and exercises to help you negotiate like a boss and get exactly what you want.

If you're an entrepreneur, it's important to understand that selling is a skillset. It's not a natural ability that you are born with. You have to learn how to sell. And while you may not be able to control whether someone buys your product or service, you can control the way you sell it.

What if you could have the inside scoop on some of the world's best negotiators and negotiation coaches? What if you could master the art of negotiation like a boss, anywhere, anytime, and with anyone?

In this new book, I reveal the secrets behind the negotiation methods of some of the world's top-performing sales professionals and the world's most influential negotiation coaches. The techniques I teach will help you increase your income, increase your personal and professional relationships, and improve your business results, no matter who you're negotiating with or where you happen to be when you negotiate.

In this book, you'll learn how to approach negotiation and build rapport like a boss. You'll discover the best ways to engage, persuade, and close any deal, regardless of the size. You'll be able to negotiate with anyone—even your competitors, bosses, employees, partners, and family—and you'll be able to do so without losing respect or alienating people. Plus, you'll gain insight and techniques to build rapport and become a much better conversationalist and negotiator. If you're a leader in your organization, you'll be able to negotiate more effectively and get better results—and have fun doing it.

In this book, you'll learn:

- How to identify your negotiating style and use it to your advantage.
- How to set the right expectations before you start negotiating.
- How to ask questions to gather information and build rapport.
- The best strategies to persuade others.
- How to listen and make others feel comfortable.
- How to close the deal and keep everyone happy.
- How to win arguments and debates.
- How to avoid being trapped in a negotiation.
- How to work with different personalities and personality types.
- How to deal with people who don't want to

negotiate or just want to "win".
- How to deal with common negotiating mistakes.
- How to get the most out of a negotiation.

You'll also learn how to negotiate when you're under pressure, whether you're negotiating with your boss, your children, your spouse, your employees, or your competitors. You'll learn how to make sure you're comfortable while you're negotiating.

You've got an opportunity to be a rock star negotiator in business today. But if you're just doing the same old thing, you're not going to succeed at negotiating like a rock star. You have to change your mindset, your expectations, and your negotiation tactics.

If you want to become a master negotiator, you have to put yourself into the shoes of a CEO, COO, CFO, VP of Sales, CMO, and all other senior executives. You have to understand their priorities, their needs, their desires, and how to build relationships with them.

That's why I wrote this book – to show you how to sell like titans and make your negotiations more effective and less stressful; a new approach to negotiation that allows you to become a world-class negotiator and expert in any situation.

This book in the **Sell Like Titans** series is for anyone who negotiates or has ever wished they could negotiate like a boss. It's also about changing the way you think, act, and feel when negotiating.

Chapter 1

Understanding the Art of Negotiation

Many of us like to think we're born negotiators. But most of us really suck at negotiating. We don't realize how much better we could be at negotiating if only we had an improved understanding of the psychology behind negotiations. In fact, I've learned that all my negotiating abilities (or lack thereof) revolve around two primary concepts: <u>I have an expectation and a preference. My expectation is based on what I want and need. My preference is based on what I think is possible.</u>

In this chapter, I'm going to share with you some of the psychological principles that explain why we often make bad decisions in negotiations. I'm also going to give you some simple tactics that will help you to improve your negotiating skills.

The biggest mistake people make when they negotiate is that they try to change others' preferences and expectations. Instead, what you should do is change your own. You should focus on changing your own preferences and expectations. Changing other people's preferences and expectations is tricky because you're not always sure whether their preferences and expectations are what they really want and need. If someone tells you that she wants something, but it's not what she needs, then you'll have trouble persuading her to change her mind.

When it comes to negotiations, I'm a big fan of changing my own expectations and preferences. When I'm negotiating with a person who I believe to be reasonable and I'm able to come up with a good outcome for both of us, I'm happy. But when the negotiation ends in failure, I don't feel bad. It's because I didn't change my own expectations and preferences.

If you want to improve your negotiating skills, you need to change your own expectations and preferences. If you want to improve your negotiation skills, you need to think differently about what you want and need. I'm not saying that you should always negotiate in the best interest of others. In fact, I believe that you should do everything you can to serve yourself first. But you should also consider what others need. When you focus on changing your own expectations and preferences, you're able to change other people's as well.

Negotiation is when two or more parties agree on the terms

of a deal. This doesn't mean you're forced to give up everything you want. It means that you and the other party are in agreement about what you want, and what you can accept. In an ideal situation, each party wins what they want while everyone walks away satisfied. But it's possible to win something without having to give up anything of value. So how can you negotiate something you want while holding on to what you need?

The answer lies in the art of compromise. You can use compromise to get what you want while keeping your needs and desires intact. <u>Compromise is not a dirty word in business, compromise is a two-way street. One side has to make concessions, but both sides have to be happy with the outcome. If one side is unhappy with the outcome, then the compromise isn't worth it.</u> This is true in personal life as well. It's possible to compromise, but if you can't both get what you want, then you don't really win. In personal relationships, compromise can be a way of getting along and working together. Compromising means giving up something you need in order to get something else you want. But that doesn't mean you have to give up everything you want. You can get what you need, while still holding on to what you need. Compromise is the process of coming to an agreement on terms. You negotiate by exchanging things you want for other things you need. This is a two-step process.

First, you need to identify the thing you want, the thing you need, and the things you compromise on. Then you try to come to an agreement on how to go about getting each of those things. In business, you use compromise to build relationships. In personal life, you use compromise to get along with your spouse or significant other. Compromise is not always easy in business, it's necessary to compromise on some things.

There are times when you have to give up something you want in order to get something you need. But there are times when it's not necessary to compromise. Sometimes, it's better to have the thing you want and not need than to have the thing you need and do not want. For example, when you buy a new car, it's good to have the new car, but if you have to pay a lot of money for it, then you may as well not buy it. It's better to buy a car, but not pay a lot of money for it. That way, you're getting the car and saving some money at the same time. Sometimes, the way you get the thing you want is by compromising on other things.

While many people may think that negotiation is only used in business or politics, it can be used to negotiate nearly anything in life. Whether it's trying to secure a better rate for your rental car, convincing your boss that you deserve a raise, or just making sure to get a discount on a product you want to purchase, negotiation is a skill that everyone should practice at some point in their life. Whether you're negotiating with your landlord to lower your rent or with a potential buyer to lower the price you're asking, the key is to be prepared. Be knowledgeable about what you want and what you're willing to settle on, and always communicate clearly.

Negotiation is another area that's often glossed over in the world of online marketing and business development. But for most companies, negotiating contracts and pricing isn't something they're willing to invest in. It can be incredibly difficult for many companies to grasp the concept of negotiation as a tool. To negotiate effectively, you need to understand why people act the way they do and why it's beneficial for them to change their behavior. The first step is to figure out the right kind of conversation to have with the other party in a way that's useful to you. Once you understand the value of negotiation and how it works, the next step is to use the information to influence the other party to change his or her position.

The first negotiation principle is something many people know by its name but may not always use in practice. It's called ***the art of compromise***. There are two common ways to use the art of compromise in your negotiations.

The first, and easiest way, is to ask yourself what you want from the other person and agree to that. Then work toward getting that result. You might say to a potential customer that you have a couple of items available at two different prices, and if they want both you'll sell them for the higher price. This works because your customer doesn't want to spend any more money than necessary and if he or she can get both items for the same price, then he or she can afford them.

The second way to use the art of compromise is to take a position and then work toward a compromise. For example, a person who wants a $5,000 car may negotiate with a dealer by saying, "I'm willing to pay $4,000 for the car, and if you'll give me a $1,000 trade-in value, I'll buy it." The person who wants the $5,000 car agrees and gives the person a $1,000 trade-in value. This works because the dealer realizes that this person can buy a car for less than $4,000, and so he's willing to compromise for a lower price.

This second way of using the art of compromise is more difficult. You have to be willing to make compromises in order to get what you want, even if you don't want to. It takes discipline and practice.

Here are some other principles that you can use when negotiating:

Focus on the other person's needs: When you're negotiating with another person, you're not only trying to get your own needs met but also the needs of the other person. Asking yourself whether your needs are more important than someone else's will help you determine how to proceed. If your needs are more important, then you should take the lead and negotiate accordingly.

Don't make promises you can't keep: Most people have a tendency to promise things they know they can't deliver on. You may make a deal with a vendor by promising to send them a check for $10,000 on Friday. But if you don't have the money to pay for the $10,000 by Friday, you've made a promise you can't keep. It's easy to promise something you can't deliver because you want to be liked or because you think that you can persuade the other person to give you what you want. But if you do that, you'll lose respect. Instead, set a time frame for when you're going to fulfill your promise. This will increase your chances of getting what you want.

Don't get angry: When you negotiate with another person, you may get angry at him or her for not giving you what you want. But this will only hurt you. Anger is a strong emotion that can cause you to make decisions that are not in your best interest. As a result, you'll have a difficult time getting what you want. If you feel anger about a situation, then take a deep breath and try to control it. If you can't, then you need to talk to someone about how you're feeling.

Be willing to walk away: If you really want something and the other person won't give it to you, then you should be willing to walk away. Don't be afraid of walking away because you think you'll lose something if you do. Remember that you don't have to be in a relationship with someone in order to get what you want. If you want to use the art of compromise when negotiating, then you'll have to practice. You may have to make compromises that you don't like. But if you practice and learn from your experiences, then you'll become better at using the art of compromise. And as a result, you'll gain respect from others.

Negotiation takes skill and practice, but the end result can be very rewarding. This is especially true when you are negotiating with another business owner. The key is to listen carefully, ask questions, and take notes to build a rapport with the other party. Then offer up a counter-proposal and wait for a reaction. Don't get discouraged if the answer isn't "yes" right away. It's not about making the other person say yes, it's about listening to what he or she is telling you and taking it seriously. This may take a couple of rounds to come to a compromise.

If there's one thing that most people hate, it's negotiating. This comes in large part because there are so many people who do it poorly. To succeed in a negotiation, you need to understand your other party and know how to move the negotiation forward. The best negotiators know how to read their counterpart's behavior, which means they're able to assess how their negotiation is going. This skill is particularly helpful when you're working with someone who is very different from you. You have to be able to adapt your negotiation style to the other party and what they want to accomplish.

How to Identify Your Negotiating Style and Use it to Your Advantage

When it comes to negotiating, each of us has a unique way of thinking. Each of us has a style of negotiation that works best for us, whether it's through verbal or written communication.

Here are three important styles you should know about:

1. The Con Man: The Con Man thinks in terms of the

"what ifs". What if I ask too high? What if they say no? What if we don't sign on the dotted line? The Con Man is all about getting what he wants, without having to compromise. He doesn't like to give, but wants others to give him what he needs. He wants it now, not later. His style can be described as: <u>Rational (rationalizing his behavior), Pessimistic (always thinking the worst), Negative (always looking at the negative side of things),</u> Con Man style is most effective when you are trying to get something done quickly and don't have time to negotiate. You need to convince someone that something is a good idea. You don't want to reveal too much of your hand. You want to convince them that you are right and they are wrong. You want to make sure that you get everything that you want. The right way to approach a Con Man is to let him think about the "what ifs". You need to make sure that the Con Man is always thinking about "what ifs".

2. The Power Player: The Power Player thinks in terms of the *"I wants"*. What do I want? What's my end goal? What if I ask for too little? What if they say yes? What if we don't sign on the dotted line? The Power Player is all about getting what he wants, regardless of what others think. He doesn't like to give, but wants others to give him what he needs. He wants it now, not later. His style can be described as: <u>Rational (rationalizing his behavior), Optimistic (always thinking the best), Positive (always looking at the positive side of things)</u>, Power Player style is most effective when: You are trying to get something done quickly and don't have time to negotiate. You need to convince someone that something is a good idea. You want to make sure that you get everything that you want. The right way to approach a Power Player is to let him think about "I wants". You need to make sure that the Power Player is always thinking about "I wants".

3. The Dreamer: The Dreamer thinks in terms of the *"I shoulds"*. What if I ask too high? What if they say no? What if we don't sign on the dotted line? What if they don't like me? What if we don't work out? The Dreamer is all about getting what he wants, and having fun along the way. He doesn't like to compromise, but wants others to compromise with him. He wants it now, not later. His style can be described as: Rational (rationalizing his behavior), Optimistic (always thinking the best), Positive (always looking at the positive side of things), Dreamer style is most effective when: You are trying to get something done quickly and don't have time to negotiate. You need to convince someone that something is a good idea. You want to make sure that you get everything that you want. You are in the midst of a negotiation and want to make sure you have your way. You are very confident about what you are saying, and are not concerned about negotiating skills. You are an "I should" person, and you know that if you negotiate you will lose.

If you want to be successful in negotiations, you need to know your own negotiating style. The right style will help you get what you want in the fastest and easiest way possible.

Here are four ways to think about negotiation:
- I'm a power negotiator who believes in using my power to get what I want.
- I'm a relational negotiator who focuses on the relationship between two or more people.
- I'm a rational negotiator who thinks through every detail in order to arrive at a win-win solution.
- I'm a process negotiator who focuses on moving toward a goal.

In my experience, these four different mindsets work best when you use them together. The process mindset is helpful if you're focused on a goal that you need to achieve.

For example, I'll often start by thinking through the details of how I'm going to communicate with someone in order to reach my goals. I'll then move to the rational stage by considering what they might say in return.

When you are in a relationship, I suggest that you think through your own actions as well as the other person's reactions. I'll often start by thinking about how I might respond if I'm offended by something someone says. Then I'll consider what that person might say in response. Power negotiators can use all four approaches.

For example, I believe that I should use my power to get what I want. I can use logic and facts to justify why I want something or why I'm entitled to it. At the same time, I can also use emotion to persuade someone else to give me what I want. You may be wondering why I suggest that you use these different mindsets together. It's because they work best when you use them in this way. Using one mindset exclusively is unlikely to succeed, whereas using all four will usually work. You'll find it easier to use all four if you begin by thinking through the details of how you're going to communicate with someone in order to reach your goals. That way, you're thinking through the steps that you need to take. After that, you can move on to thinking through what that person might say in response to your actions. Then you can consider what you might say in return. The more you think about each step, the easier it will be to use each of these mindsets.

Power: *Power negotiators* focus on their own power and the power of those who are around them. Power negotiators believe that they have the right to get what they want because they have a lot of power. Power negotiators are motivated by the need to be recognized, appreciated, and liked.

Relational: *Relational negotiators* focus on the relationship between two or more people. Relational negotiators believe that if they can maintain a good relationship with others, they will be able to get what they want. Relational negotiators are motivated by the desire to be liked, respected, and accepted.

Rational: *Rational negotiators* think through every detail in order to arrive at a win-win solution. Rational negotiators believe that they can arrive at a win-win outcome through logical analysis and careful consideration. Rational negotiators are motivated by the need to make sure that they do things the right way.

Process: *Process negotiators* focus on moving toward a goal. Process negotiators believe that their actions will lead them to a win-win outcome. Process negotiators are motivated by the need to reach a particular goal.

Here's an example of each of these mindsets:

<u>Power negotiators</u> want recognition, appreciation, and a sense of being important. They often say things like, *"I'm not going to take no for an answer."*

<u>Relational negotiators</u> want to be liked, respected, and accepted. They say things like, *"I don't want to start this fight. I'll leave it up to you to decide how we move forward."*

<u>Rational negotiators</u> think through every detail in order to arrive at a win-win solution. They say things like, *"I'm

sorry if I offended you. I was just trying to get what I wanted."

Process negotiators are focused on moving toward a goal. They say things like, *"Let's try to figure out what will make us both happy."*

Types of Negotiation Styles

It's time to talk about negotiation styles. If you're a business owner, you've probably heard of "negotiation styles." They're all over the Internet, and they are everywhere. Everyone has their own way of doing things, and it's important that you find your own style. The reason is simple: you don't want to be in conflict with everyone. But before we start talking about different negotiation styles, let's first look at what they are.

What are Negotiation Styles?

Negotiation styles are basically the types of people you're likely to be negotiating with. Each one has its own strengths and weaknesses. The five most common negotiation styles are listed below.

The first is the **Authoritative style:** These people have very high self-confidence and are usually very good communicators. When they negotiate, they'll make sure that their needs are met. They will also set the terms, and if they don't get them, they'll walk away. This style can be frustrating for you because you're not going to win much of anything.

The second style is the **Amiable:** These people are more relaxed. They're willing to work things out. They're also usually very friendly, and they like people a lot. However, they have a tendency to agree to things without thinking about it. If you're in a negotiation with this person, you might find that you're agreeing to things that you shouldn't.

The third style is the **Competitive:** These people are very driven. They want to win at all costs, even if that means losing. They will fight tooth and nail to make sure that they get what they want. They'll make it very clear what they're willing to do and not do, and they will negotiate until they get what they want. They're very strong negotiators.

The fourth style is the **Analytical:** These people are

always looking for reasons why something isn't working. They'll be analyzing everything and trying to figure out the best way to do things. They're great thinkers and they're very smart. But sometimes they can be too analytical, and they'll try to control everything instead of letting other people take the lead.

Finally, there's the **Collaborative:** These people will try to work with others in order to make sure that everyone gets what they want. They'll listen to other people's ideas and work together to make sure everyone wins.

So how do you know which style you're most like? The good news is that you don't have to guess.

You can simply use the [Myers-Briggs test](https://www.truity.com/test/type-finder-personality-test-new) (visit https://www.truity.com/test/type-finder-personality-test-new) or (visit https://www.123test.com/personality-test/) to find out!

Some of the other common types of negotiation styles and personality are;

The Assertive Style – This is the most common style. It is used to demonstrate your power and ability to negotiate.

You are not afraid of confrontation, you do not like to lose and you don't like to be told no.

The Aggressive Style – This is the opposite of the Assertive Style. It is a style that is used to force your will on others. If you think you are right, then there is no need to negotiate. You are not interested in other people's opinions.

The Submissive Style – This is the style that is used when you want to please someone. It is the way you get along with everyone. It's easy, relaxed, and not so serious. The Submissive Style allows you to be yourself.

The Dominant Style – This is the style that is used when you want to dominate someone. It's hard, firm, and serious. You can take charge of a situation and you have authority. The

Authoritative Style – This is the style that is used when you want to lead someone. You are in control and can give orders. It's the most common style of leadership because it is used in most situations.

Informal Style – This is the style that is used in casual conversations. The leader takes the conversation into their own hands, and you follow along. It's a very social way of leading, and it's often used by leaders in sales or marketing.

Autocratic Style – This is the style that is used when you want to control everything.

The Agreeable Style – This is used by those who are more interested in maintaining harmony than winning. You like to keep things positive and avoid conflict at all costs.

The Collaborative Style – This is used by those who like to work with other people and have a keen interest in getting along with others. You prefer to work with others than against them.

The Indecisive Style – This is used by those who like to avoid conflict. They avoid making a decision until it is forced on them. This can be a real advantage in certain situations. But, in general, indecision is not the best way to get things done. It is often seen as a weakness and will usually make others think you are afraid of making a mistake or losing.

The Compulsive Style – This person will do whatever he or she has to do, even if it is not the right thing. If they have an important meeting, they will attend. If they have a problem, they will spend time on it. If they are trying to lose weight, they will start exercising. If they are in a relationship with someone who they care about, they will give them their all.

The Unreliable Style – This person is unreliable, and can't be counted on. They will do whatever they want whenever they want, and it will be done half-assed. They may also do things without warning, or make up excuses as to why they are not going to do something.

Negotiation styles can be learned and you can change your style of negotiation. If you feel that you are too assertive, you can learn to be more diplomatic. This is an important aspect of negotiation because if you are not assertive enough you may not get what you want.

How can you use this knowledge to negotiate better deals for yourself? The key is to figure out which side of the table you are comfortable and feel confident on and don't have any hesitation about being the aggressor or the responder. By knowing your negotiating style, you can adjust your approach to a negotiation accordingly. Knowing your own strengths and weaknesses in negotiating can help you build confidence and allow you to effectively approach and negotiate with others.

When it comes to negotiating, there are two types of people: those who negotiate and those who don't. Those who negotiate understand that in order to make a deal work, they need to come to an agreement on both sides. Those who don't negotiate understand that sometimes, in order to get what they want, they need to take something from someone else. What does this mean for you? It means that if you're not comfortable with either side of the table, you need to find a way to be comfortable on both sides of the negotiation. This may mean that you need to be willing to go in with a clear objective and ask for more than you think you deserve. Or it may mean that you need to be willing to walk away from a deal if you're not getting what you want. Regardless of what you're asking for or what you're willing to give up, the key to negotiating is being open to hearing another person's point of view and being able to compromise.

How to Set the Right Expectations before You Start Negotiating

You have to be aware of the fact that the consumer is not always in the same state as you are. Even if they are in a hurry, they may be more willing to wait. They might be anxious to buy, but they might also be fearful of buying too soon. The key here is to figure out what your potential consumer needs and wants. And then match those with what you're offering, in a way that makes them comfortable.

The first step in doing this is to figure out what they need, and how they feel about the product or service. You can use a tool like the **Customer Decision Model (CDM)**, which helps you understand what it is your potential consumer is looking for and why. This will give you an idea of their emotional state, and where they might be vulnerable. Once you've done this, it's time to set up a dialogue with them, and start talking about your product or service. This is one of the most important steps in the entire negotiation process. It gives you the opportunity to talk about what they want and how they think about their needs. If you can do this successfully, you will build a relationship with your potential customer that will make it easier for you to sell them whatever it is that you're selling. If you're not aware of their needs and wants, you will end up wasting both your time and theirs. When you start talking to them, you should be asking questions about their needs and wants.

It's not enough to say, "We have a product that will solve your problems." You have to figure out exactly what those problems are, and how they will benefit from the solution you're offering. Setting the right expectations is an important part of the process. You need to set the right expectations before you start negotiating, so you don't waste your time or theirs. If you're negotiating with a consumer, they need to understand the cost of the service or product you're offering them. It doesn't matter if it's a large or small business. In most cases, the cost of a service or product is one of the first things that a potential customer will ask about. It's also one of the first things that they'll compare to see if they can find something cheaper somewhere else. If you don't know what they're looking for, or how much it costs, you can end up wasting both their time and yours. This is because you might end up spending your time trying to get them to agree to a price that they can't afford. You'll also be wasting their time because they'll just walk away.

The same goes for when you're negotiating with a supplier. You have to understand how much money you're paying for what you want, and you have to know what your potential supplier's costs are. If you're negotiating with a supplier, you need to know the cost of the product or service you're buying. You also need to know what the cost of the product or service is in the market. This will give you an idea of what you should be asking for.

> *"Don't expect to walk into any negotiation without having done your homework."*

"It's not that hard, but it takes discipline to prepare and to know how to play your cards." When you're preparing for a negotiation, you have to think about what you need and what you don't need. What are the risks and costs of you walking away from the negotiation? If you need something right away and you don't think you can get it, are there ways you can stretch your budget to accommodate the need and still get it done? Once you've got a clear view of what you need, you can focus on what you can offer to get that thing. For example, you can offer discounts or freebies to entice someone to agree to give you what you need.

If you don't understand what you need in a negotiation, you'll be in for a rude awakening. This is where you need to be clear about what you need in the negotiation and how much it will cost to get that need met. Don't be afraid to walk away from the negotiation if you don't think you can meet your needs with the resources available.

I'm often asked if it's better to ask for what you want or to tell someone what you want. The answer is both *yes and no*. It depends on the situation and the person you're dealing with. In a negotiation, you're asking for something that costs money. If you ask for something without knowing what you need, you may not be able to pay for it. This can be costly in more ways than one. If you have a clear idea of what you need, you can make sure you can afford it. You can also avoid wasting time negotiating if you know what you want and don't need to spend time negotiating for things you don't need.

On the flip side, if you don't ask for what you need, you'll end up with something you don't need and may not even be able to afford. What do you want? You can ask yourself what you want in a negotiation. Some people are naturally good at this and some aren't. If you're unsure about what you want, you can start by listing things that you think would make the negotiation better.

Ask yourself what you'd like to get out of the negotiation. Is it better to get more money or a better deal? Is it better to get a free lunch or an hour off? Do you want more time or to have a smaller bill? There are many ways to answer these questions. It's helpful to know what you want before you negotiate. You can also ask for what you need. You may want to say something like, *"I'm not sure how much time I need, but I know I want a discount on my bill."* You can also ask for what you need in a negotiation. This can be helpful in getting the best deal. It will also help you avoid wasting time negotiating for things you don't need. When it comes to negotiating, you should never take anything personally. Negotiating is a skill that everyone can learn. In fact, it's the only skill that can be learned.

There are many books and classes available that can teach you how to negotiate effectively. But, even if you're good at negotiating, there are some things you can do to make sure you get what you want out of a negotiation. Negotiating isn't easy. Sometimes, it's easier to just get what you want and not have to negotiate.

Here are 8 tips for negotiating that will help you get what you want out of every negotiation.

1. **Be Prepared Negotiating requires preparation:** It's important that you know what you want and what you're willing to give up. If you don't have a clear understanding of what you want and what you're willing to give up, it's hard to negotiate effectively. You'll be more successful when you've prepared in advance.

2. **Listen Carefully:** When you're listening, pay attention to the words people are saying. Pay attention to the non-verbal cues they use. People who are trying to deceive you will show signs of deception.

3. **Ask Questions:** If someone is telling you something,

you should ask questions. If you're unsure about a statement, you should ask for clarification. If someone is giving you an ultimatum, you should ask for more information.

4. **Show Respect:** It's important that you show respect during negotiations. When you respect your opponent, you'll find yourself more willing to compromise and agree to their demands.

5. **Use Humor:** When you're negotiating, it's important to make the other person laugh. Make them smile and you'll be more likely to get what you want out of the negotiation.

6. **Be Clear on Your Terms:** You should have clear terms before you start negotiating. If the other party doesn't understand your terms, they'll be more likely to walk away from the negotiation.

7. **Know Your Goals:** You should know what your goals are before you begin negotiating. It's important that you don't go into negotiations without having a clear idea of

what you want.

8. **Negotiate with Dignity:** You should negotiate with dignity. When you negotiate with dignity, you'll find yourself more successful when you're negotiating. There are many ways you can become a better negotiator. By using the tips and information in this book, you'll be able to improve your ability to negotiate effectively.

How to Ask Questions to Gather Information and Build Rapport

We all have that one friend who talks too much. And yet, there's something about someone who asks questions that makes people like us open up. According to researchers, asking questions can make you appear friendly and approachable, and people are likely to like you more because of it. So why not ask questions of others to build rapport and establish relationships?

People often assume that asking questions is a sign of weakness. But, according to the Journal of Personality and Social Psychology, asking questions is actually an effective way to build rapport with others.

Here's what you need to know: Ask questions that show interest in another person When you ask a question, it shows that you want to know more about the other person. You might say something like, "I don't know much about you. What do you do for fun?" The key is to make your questions seem genuine. When people feel that they can trust you, they're more likely to share information with you.

1. Start conversations by asking open-ended questions Instead of making your conversation about yourself, try starting with a question that invites someone else to talk. For example, ask, *"What's going on at work?" or "How's the weather been lately?"* These types of questions give people a chance to tell their stories and share what they think about a particular topic.

2. Ask about what's important to the other person. When you ask a question about what another person is interested in, you're giving them a chance to show off their interests. It's a great way to start a conversation because it allows you to find common ground and build rapport.

3. Ask questions that make people feel comfortable
   When you ask questions, it shows that you're interested in learning about the other person. People feel more comfortable with someone who shows that they want to know more about them. If you're having trouble starting conversations with new people, try asking open-ended questions that make the person feel comfortable.
4. Listen closely to understand what the other person is saying. Asking questions is one thing; listening is another. You need to pay attention to what others are saying so you can give them a chance to talk about themselves. You might say something like, "I really like your story about your family vacation." Or, "What does that song mean to you?" Listen for key words and phrases, such as, "that's a great idea." You can use these words to follow up and ask more questions.
5. Don't assume that everyone is interested in talking with you. If someone doesn't seem interested in talking to you, don't take it personally. It's common for people to be shy when they first meet someone. It's okay to try asking questions again if you don't

get a response the first time. It takes practice to start conversations with new people, but the more you practice, the easier it will become.

6. Don't force conversations. The more comfortable you are with someone, the less you'll have to say. People appreciate it when you let them talk about themselves without interrupting them or forcing them to talk about you.

7. Learn how to respond to questions. Once you understand the questions that people are asking you, you can learn how to answer them. When you know what people want to hear from you, you can use that information to prepare an answer.

8. Be confident and assertive. Sometimes you can avoid awkward situations by being confident and assertive. Confident people tend to make better conversational partners because they don't hesitate to say what they think.

In a survey study conducted by a marketing research firm called **Opinium**, consumers said they'd rather be asked questions than be given a list of options to choose from. Opinium conducted a similar study last year that showed just how strong this desire is: 74% of respondents said that asking people questions was more persuasive than giving them choices. Asking the right questions is an essential element of communication; it gives you valuable information and builds rapport between you and your audience.

Here are a few questions to keep in mind while creating content, product, or selling and gathering information:

- What do you like about our product?
- What makes our product unique?
- What's your biggest challenge with our product?
- What do you dislike about our product?
- How can we make your life easier?
- What do you want to see in future versions?
- What should we add to the product?
- What changes should we make?
- What could we improve?

You can use these questions to gather information about your audience. This will help you tailor your content and messaging appropriately, and it will also help you create a better experience for your audience in order to sell like titans.

Chapter 2

How to Turn a Negotiating Tactic into a Strategic Advantage

Sometimes you just have to take advantage of the situation you find yourself in, and sometimes that situation is a negotiation. Whether the stakes are high or low, negotiating can be an effective way to gain an advantage and move toward your goal. You can use it to turn a negotiation into a strategic advantage.

The goal of this chapter is to help you turn a simple tactical negotiation tactic into a strategic one. In many situations, if you ask for the other side's best offer, they will be forced to make an offer that is better than they wanted to make before you asked for it. You can turn this into a strategic advantage by not asking for their best offer. Instead, you should ask them to make an offer that is better than they wanted to make before you asked them to make it. They will not be able to say no. This tactic is a simple one. It requires you to have a certain level of understanding of what makes people tick. If you don't know anything about the other side, you will need to learn some things. It will take some effort to get to this point. The first step is to understand why you want to use this tactic.

I recommend that you have a clear picture of your goal in mind before you go any further. In addition, you will need to have some understanding of the other side's goals and motivations.

Why not ask for their best offer?

The reason that you should not ask for the other side's best offer is that it may lead to an *impasse*. An impasse occurs when one side has no interest in making an offer that is better than the one it was already willing to make. If you ask for their best offer and they are unwilling to make a concession, you are going to have to find another way to get what you want.

If you've ever been in negotiations, you know how hard it can be to get your message across, especially if you're trying to persuade someone that you can do something for them better than anyone else. But sometimes, there are ways to make the other party feel like they have no choice but to accept your offer.

Here's one such tactic: *Ask yourself what the other side wants*. Chances are, it's what you want, too. Once you understand what the other party wants, use that information to make them feel like they have no other option but to agree to your terms.

Tell them you want what they want. You may think you don't care about the other person's wishes, but the truth is, you probably do. If you really don't, you wouldn't be so quick to jump on a deal. But since you're going to be working with the other party, you need to put their interests first. This is where asking yourself what they want comes in handy. By asking yourself what they want, you can learn more about the situation and what they're willing to accept, making it easier for you to get what you want. And if you really don't care about their wishes, why should they?

Sometimes we need to take the initiative and go above and beyond the call of duty to help others succeed. That's what's known as *"negotiating from strength."*

When you're negotiating with someone who is stronger than you are, you can increase your leverage by doing the following:

1. Make sure that you're dealing with a person who values his or her time. People who value their time don't want to

waste it.

2. Focus on what's in it for them. They're trying to maximize their results, so make sure that your offer is something they want.

3. Be willing to say "no." You can't always say no, but that doesn't mean you have to be rude or insensitive when you do it.

4. If you're stuck between a rock and a hard place, ask yourself what you can do to make it easier for the other party to agree. Then, do your best to help them reach that point.

5. Remember that if you make the other party feel strong and confident, you'll get more out of the negotiation.

6. Be open to new ideas. A good negotiator will look at the situation from a different angle.

7. Be patient. It takes time to get the other party to see things from your perspective.

8. Be willing to negotiate on their terms. Don't force the other party to come to your terms.

9. Be flexible. You need to be open to change and willing to compromise.

10. Don't take the bait. When you sense that the other party is about to throw a curve ball, back off. They may be

trying to distract you so that you make a mistake.

11. Let them lead. When you're in a negotiation, let the other party lead you by responding to what they say rather than what you want.

12. Keep your cool. If you get too emotional or angry, the other party won't listen.

13. Have a backup plan. No matter how hard you try, sometimes things don't go as planned. If you have a backup plan, you'll be able to respond more effectively if things don't go your way.

14. Be willing to walk away. Sometimes you just can't reach an agreement. If this happens, be willing to walk away and look for a better deal elsewhere.

15. Be willing to make concessions. If you need something from the other party, be willing to make concessions so that you can get what you want.

16. Don't be afraid to ask for help. If you need to negotiate with someone who has more experience than you do, ask for their help.

17. Ask yourself what you can do to make the other party feel strong and confident. Then, do your best to help them feel this way.

Don't forget to use some creativity. Negotiating isn't a bad thing; it's just that most people who start negotiations do it without thinking strategically.

To really be successful in negotiating, you have to be strategic. To win business, you need to be in the right place at the right time. And you need to have the right pitch and the right price. But there's one more thing that matters: the way you approach your negotiation. The key is to find a strategic advantage in the negotiation. Think about your goals when negotiating. Will you be negotiating for a specific project, or looking for a long-term relationship? Once you've identified your goal, be very clear about your expectations in the negotiation and what will happen if you don't meet them.

If you're doing a project with a new client, you might want to negotiate the terms of the contract. If you're looking for a long-term relationship, think about whether you're willing to pay for a longer contract than your competitor offers. The point is to make sure you understand the other person's goals and are clear about yours. Then you can figure out a strategy that puts you in the driver's seat.

How to Get the Most out of a Negotiation

There are two approaches to negotiating: the *"my way or the highway"* approach and the *"both of us get something out of it"* approach. The first is more common, but in reality, the second is often the only way to get anything done. So, if you are using the my-way-or-the-highway approach, you are missing out on a lot of possibilities.

The my-way-or-the-highway approach says that one side should never compromise and always insist on what they want. This approach leads to a lot of frustration and wasted time because the other party always ends up saying no. In reality, this is an unrealistic approach.

In business, there are times when both sides need to compromise in order to come to an agreement. This is where the *both-of-us-get-something-out-of-it* approach comes in.

In a negotiation, both sides should be willing to compromise and accept something less than what they want in order to reach an agreement. When you are negotiating with another person, the best way to do this is to give them what they want now, but ask for something in return later. If you are able to negotiate with the other person in this way, you can usually get more of what you want and still have something left over. This is one of the reasons why the *both-of-us-get-something-out-of-it* approach works so well. You give the other party what they want, but you ask for something in return. If you do this, you will get a lot more out of the deal than if you just insist on getting everything that you want now. The other party will often feel that they owe you something and will agree to your request.

Another reason that the *both-of-us-get-something-out-of-it* approach works so well is that it keeps you from feeling that you have given up everything to get something. If you give the other party what they want now, but ask for something in return, they are not going to feel like they have given up anything because they are still getting something out of the negotiation. This also allows you to feel good about yourself because you are willing to compromise and accept less than what you want now in order to get more of what you want later.

The last reason that the *both-of-us-get-something-out-of-it* approach works so well is that it allows you to leave the negotiation feeling that you got the better deal. If you are able to negotiate with the other party in this way, they will feel that they have gotten a lot more out of the deal than if you just insisted on getting everything that you wanted. This will make them feel like they got a great deal and will make it easier for them to feel like they owe you something. This is one of the reasons why the *both-of-us-get-something-out-of-it* approach works so well.

There are three main things to remember when using the *both-of-us-get-something-out-of-it* approach.

First, you should try to give the other person what they want now, but ask for something in return later.

Second, you should always be willing to compromise and accept less than what you want now in order to get more of what you want later.

Finally, you should always leave the negotiation feeling that you got the better deal.

If you are able to negotiate with the other party in this way, they will feel that they have gotten a great deal, and will make it easier for them to feel that they owe you something.

This will make them feel like they owe you something and will make it easier for them to feel good about themselves. This will make it easier for you to leave the negotiation feeling that you got the better deal.

In order to use the *both-of-us-get-something-out-of-it* approach, you need to learn how to ask for what you want without being too demanding. You should also know how to be flexible and willing to compromise. In addition, you should be honest and admit when you are not willing to compromise. If you are able to do this, you can usually get a lot more out of the negotiation than if you just insist on getting everything that you want now.

How to Manage Yourself During a Negotiation

Negotiations involve communication skills that are often overlooked. You need to think like a negotiator and communicate like a salesman. A big part of successful negotiations is preparation. Research what you want to ask for, how much value you are willing to offer, and what you are willing to sacrifice, and then come up with a strategy for achieving your goals.

Negotiating is often one of the most stressful parts of being in business. But even though you may feel the pressure of a negotiation, you don't need to lose your cool. If you want to have a successful negotiation, you have to be able to control your emotions and manage yourself during the process. As a leader, it is important to be able to show empathy towards your counterpart and be patient, especially if you feel your negotiation is a losing situation. It's not just negotiations that you'll have to manage yourself during the process, but any kind of meeting. We need to take care of ourselves and our minds. Whether it's because we're tense or nervous, our body language can say a lot. Body language says a lot about how we're feeling and how we perceive people around us. Being prepared, and staying present, can help us manage our own stress and our emotions during the meeting.

Negotiations can be nerve-wracking for both parties involved. And yet the end result is often a successful outcome. The key to negotiating successfully is to understand what's happening in the negotiation from the beginning, not only what's happening during the actual negotiation. So, how should you manage yourself and prepare for negotiations?

Here are some tips:

1. **Plan Ahead:** Before you even get started on the negotiation, you need to know what you want to accomplish. You need to know what you are going to ask for, how much value you want to offer, and what you are willing to sacrifice. Then you need to come up with a strategy for achieving your goals.

2. **Get Comfortable:** The more comfortable you are in the negotiation, the better off you'll be. Be sure to have your phone on you, be prepared with paper and pens, and be comfortable in your own skin. If you're uncomfortable, you'll be hesitant to speak up or give up something that you want to keep.

3. **Stay Positive:** Being positive during negotiations can help you stay calm, even when you're stressed out. Focus on the good things that will happen after you've reached a compromise. Instead of focusing on the negatives, focus on the positives. This can help you stay calm and in control.

4. **Manage Your Emotions:** When you feel stressed out

or nervous, your emotions can affect your body language. If you're feeling tense, your body will tense up and you may find yourself fidgeting. If you're feeling nervous, your hands may be clammy. It is important to manage your emotions. Think about how you want to appear and what you want to communicate to your counterpart. How can you show them that you are in control?

5. **Set Boundaries:** During a negotiation, it's important to set boundaries so that you don't lose control. You don't need to agree with everything that your counterpart says or does. Set boundaries to ensure that you stay in control and that you do not get lost in the conversation.

6. **Keep in Mind the Time Frame:** Negotiations can last for hours, or they can end in less than five minutes. This can be nerve-wracking because it's hard to keep track of time when you are in a negotiation. Make sure you have something to write down so that you don't miss anything. It is important to stay on track during the negotiation. If you don't know what you want, then how can you expect to reach an agreement?

7. **Be Clear About What You Want:** If you want to negotiate with your counterpart, you have to be clear about what you want. Don't try to negotiate on something that you don't understand. It is important to ask questions if you don't understand something.

8. **Be Present:** Negotiations are often stressful. It's easy to get distracted by what's happening around you and get caught up in the moment. Negotiations are not a race. They are a process. You can't just keep talking without listening. Make sure you listen and take notes throughout the negotiation. This will help you stay focused and organized.

9. **Give Up Something:** The last thing you want to do is give up something that you want to keep. It is important to keep your eye on the prize. You need to stay calm and focused during the negotiation. If you feel that you have no leverage, then you may want to compromise. But you have to be willing to make a sacrifice. You need to stay calm and collected so that you can negotiate successfully. Negotiating is a skill that can be learned. By practicing negotiating with different people, you can learn how to

manage yourself during negotiations. You can practice with your employees and your family. It is important to understand what you want to achieve and what you are willing to compromise. You can't be afraid to negotiate. Negotiations are an essential part of the business.

How to Deal with People Who Don't Want to Negotiate or Just Want to "Win"

If someone asks you to do something they don't want to do, they're trying to control you. Most people just want a fair exchange and to feel as if they are being respected. Even if they aren't feeling respected, if they feel like they have control, they are much more likely to do something. So, if they tell you no, ask them why. Don't argue, ask questions, or try to persuade them to do something else. Just keep asking until you get to the root of why they don't want to do it. When you have a tough customer to deal with, a little research and a few simple questions can help you find out what's going on beneath the surface. Do they just want to win? Are they feeling threatened? Are they being irrational? By understanding your customer's feelings and motivations, you'll be able to adjust your approach.

You may be tempted to use negotiation techniques to make your customer change their mind. But there are some things you should avoid, like offering too many concessions or arguing with them. If you give too much away, they may think that you're weak, or worse, that you don't value what they have to offer. When you start a negotiation by trying to convince someone to do something, you're probably not going to get very far. If someone wants to "win" a negotiation, they'll usually ask for more than what you want to give up.

So, if you negotiate with them, you'll lose. Instead, be direct. Say *"No" or "Not yet"* and ask them why. Most people will tell you why they don't want to do it. They might say that they just want to win, that they don't want to lose, or that they don't feel comfortable with the situation. By getting to the root of the problem, you can figure out how to respond. Once you understand their feelings, you can deal with them better. And remember, you can't change someone's mind if they don't have one. If you want someone to do something, you need to make it clear that you respect their opinion. Sometimes, you may get resistance from a customer because you don't know what their expectations are. If you're in a service or sales situation, you'll likely have more control over your customers than in other industries. You can ask what they expect from the relationship, or you can learn more about their needs and feelings. If you ask, they'll tell you. It's not always easy, but most people will tell you if they want something. It may seem like common sense, but when you're dealing with customers, there are a lot of things that you don't know. So, if you're just starting out, or if you have little experience, it's best to be prepared.

Read up on negotiation techniques discussed in this book, and try to use them as soon as possible. Don't make assumptions.

When it comes to sales negotiations, many people just want to win. They don't want to give up any ground, they want everything to be fixed and final at the end of the day, they just want to be done with it. There are two problems with this approach. The first is that it's very hard to get what you want. If you don't have a strong negotiation mindset, then you'll likely just be the person who always says yes. If you do have a strong negotiation mindset, then you'll probably find yourself saying no, or you might even say no in an aggressive way that doesn't help you.

The second problem is that the other party will see right through your weakness. They will see that you are not willing to negotiate and will take advantage of this fact. They will know that you're just going to accept their offer, and if they ever change the terms, you won't be able to say anything. In short, you'll lose out on a great opportunity. This is why it's important to adopt a strong negotiation mindset. The best negotiators are always looking for ways to improve their deals. They realize that the other side has something they want too, so they make a counteroffer, or they ask questions that get them more information about what the other side wants. It's not easy to be a good negotiator. It takes time and effort to learn how to do it well. But the payoff can be huge.

Negotiating is a skill that takes practice. If you don't have experience negotiating or want to just "win," then start with small deals. Start with the smallest possible dollar amount you could win in a negotiation, but still think you're making progress. After that, you should negotiate with people who have more experience, people who understand that negotiations can be fun. But if you're looking for a more serious way to get experience in the art of negotiating, then you need to start with larger deals. Start with $20,000 and $50,000.

Make sure you know your offer, your counter-offer, and the other person's counter-offer. Know how to win the deal. Know how to lose the deal. And when you do lose, don't just throw in the towel. Keep working with the other person until you get a better deal. I'm not talking about being an asshole in a negotiation. I'm talking about being realistic, being fair, and getting a good deal. Negotiating can be fun if you learn to do it right. The key is to learn how to win the deal. If you can't win the deal, then you'll have no fun.

One of the best techniques I've seen in the past couple of years for dealing with people who just want to "win" is to offer up a compromise. This is something that both sides can agree to. This is a win-win situation.

Chapter 3

How to Prepare for a Negotiation

To prepare for a negotiation, start by getting into the proper mindset, says Samuel.

One of the most important aspects of any negotiation is preparation. If you're unprepared, there's a good chance you'll come across as unprepared, too. Whether you're negotiating for yourself or trying to help others negotiate better, having a plan is critical to your success. It should include a few steps to get you started: Ask questions and clarify any details that aren't clear to you, write down key points, and keep track of who's saying what.

Before negotiating, put yourself in a position where you feel comfortable being open to new ideas. Remember, most people are not comfortable being open to ideas that they don't already agree with. The key is to be comfortable expressing your opinions, even if you don't agree with them.

The first step to preparing for a negotiation is to create an environment where you can speak openly about your ideas and feelings. This means removing any possible roadblocks that may prevent you from expressing your opinions. For example, if you are afraid of confrontation or rejection, you may want to prepare by spending some time alone or talking to friends who you trust. You should also take a few deep breaths before starting a negotiation.

Determine Your Position When it comes to preparing for a negotiation, it is important to have a clear idea of where you stand. When you are trying to reach a compromise, you should not be afraid to state what you believe is true. Don't feel like you have to justify your position or defend your ideas. The more you do this, the easier it will be to create a compromise that works for everyone involved.

If you are in a situation where you need to make a decision on behalf of someone else, then you need to start by thinking about how you would like to be treated. This means being open to others' ideas and opinions. If you have an issue with something someone says, then try and focus on why they are saying it instead of criticizing their argument. You can use this technique to avoid having a heated argument with someone who has different opinions than you.

Create a mental model; once you have prepared for

negotiation by removing any roadblocks that may prevent you from expressing your ideas and feelings, it is time to create a mental model of your negotiation. It is important to have a mental model because it will help you see the situation from the other person's point of view. This will allow you to prepare for the negotiation without getting emotionally involved. Start by putting yourself in the other person's shoes. Then imagine what you want to achieve during the negotiation. Think about what you would like to see as a result of the negotiation. Do you want to get something done? Or do you just want to make a point or tell someone what you think about them? This will help you determine how you want to approach the negotiation.

Be Flexible When it comes to preparing for a negotiation, it is important to be flexible. If you are not flexible, then you will not be able to come up with a compromise that works for everyone involved. The key to being flexible is to have an open mind. If you have already made up your mind about what you want, then you will not be open to new ideas. If you have an opinion about something, then you should not be afraid to share it. You should try to avoid making your decision based on what you think other people will think about it. Instead, you should decide what you believe is right and then see if there is a way to convince others that you are right. When it comes to preparing for a negotiation, you should never feel like you have to make concessions or take a loss in order to get a win. If you do this, then you will end up losing the negotiation. In order to get a win, you need to find a way to give up less than you would have otherwise.

Be Honest When preparing for a negotiation, it is important to be honest. If you are not honest, then you will not be able to come up with a compromise that works for everyone involved. If you are not being honest with yourself, then you will be dishonest with other people.

This can cause problems because it will force you to lie to others. When you prepare for a negotiation, you should not be afraid of making mistakes.

You should focus on creating a plan of action instead of worrying about the results. You should also think about how you want to present yourself during the negotiation. If you act nervous or overly confident, then you may come across as arrogant or annoying.

How to Deal with Common Negotiating Mistakes

Negotiation is often perceived as a zero-sum game. In reality, however, you have to take into consideration your own personal goals in addition to the other party's. For example, if your goal is to close a deal, the other party can give something up as long as it's worth more to them than to you. So, instead of focusing on what the other party is giving up, focus on what you're gaining. That's why knowing what you want and what the other party wants are crucial to making any deal work.

When you want to negotiate something (like a price) with someone, there are a couple of mistakes you can easily make. Whether you're negotiating with a vendor or employee, common negotiating mistakes can really cost you.

So, I've pulled together a list negotiation mistakes that most people make. The most common are making too many concessions, forgetting to consider the other person's position, overpromising, or failing to explain your position clearly.

1. **You need to focus on your goal:** What's your reason for asking for the deal you're seeking? This is the reason you're giving the other party. Once you have that, you can decide what you want to get out of the deal, and how to say it.

2. **Don't come in too strong:** Unless you're dealing with an inexperienced buyer, there's no need to come in too strong. If the negotiation starts off too strong, they'll never cave, and you'll never close the deal. You also want to try and be patient. It's a long game, so don't be too quick to make demands.

3. **Be a gracious winner:** In other words, you want to let your opponent know you're happy with the deal you did make, even if it's not the one you wanted. You can do this by saying, "Oh, that's perfect. I'm really glad you think so." That way, they'll be more likely to think well of you in the future.

4. **You can't force someone to like you:** If you're trying to close a deal with someone who doesn't want to work with you, there are a couple of ways to handle this. One is to try and change their mind, and the other is to just accept that you're not going to get anywhere with them.

5. **Don't try to out-negotiate someone:** If you're trying to get a better price from a seller, you're going to have to be patient. The seller is in a tough situation because they're trying to make a profit, but they don't want to lose money on it. You need to understand that, and be prepared to wait until they make a move.

6. **Don't be a pushover:** In order to close a deal, you have to be willing to walk away if you can't get what you want. That means being firm, and not agreeing to things you know you can't deliver on.

7. **Be honest:** If you're telling someone something they don't want to hear, then you need to be honest. If you're saying you want this, but it's not going to work for them, then you need to let them know.

8. **Don't make promises you can't keep:** If you say you'll do something, you need to be able to deliver. If you can't, then you need to find a different solution.

9. **Don't fall into the trap of *"You're making me feel bad, so I'm going to make you feel good"*:** You shouldn't try and make someone else feel bad if you're the one doing something wrong.

10. **Don't give away the store:** The worst thing you can do is tell someone exactly what they want to hear, and then

not follow through with it.

11. **You can't get mad if they don't like you:** You have to accept that people are not going to like you all the time.

12. **Don't try to be too nice:** If you're trying to be nice in order to get something from someone, they're not going to be impressed.

13. **Don't let them make you feel bad:** If they make you feel bad about yourself, you're never going to be able to get them to change their mind.

One of the most common mistakes business people make in negotiations is not knowing the rules. Once you know what those rules are, it will make things easier.

Another mistake is people not getting their needs met. Most negotiation scenarios start with a customer presenting the problem—the problem is what the customer wants solved. Then the client starts listing requirements to solve the problem. After that, the client may offer something different from what the customer had hoped for. If that happens, both parties lose. When you present a solution to someone else's problem, you need to be very clear about the cost of that solution in terms of what you get in return. You can't promise more than that, because the customer is under no obligation to pay you what you're asking for.

How to Avoid Being Trapped in a Negotiation

It's easy to get stuck in a negotiation if you're not sure of your next step. This is especially true when you're the one who wants something more. Here's how to avoid being trapped:

1. **Prepare yourself for what's going to happen:** Know exactly what the other party is looking for in the negotiation. Know what your counterparty is willing to give up in order to get what he or she wants.

2. **Give the other party a fair chance to negotiate:** Don't jump in and tell them what you want. Allow the other party to state what he or she needs or wants in the negotiation.

3. **Be clear on what you're offering:** Before you enter into a negotiation, decide what your counterparty is getting and what you're giving up.

4. **State what you're offering clearly and concisely:** Tell them how you're going to compensate them for what they're giving up. Explain why you're giving up what

you're giving up. This helps people feel secure about making decisions and it makes them more likely to agree with your requests.

5. **Keep an open mind:** Don't close off any possibilities. If you're open to negotiating, then you're in the right mindset for the negotiation.

6. **Have a backup plan:** Have a plan B, C, D, and E if things don't go your way. You never know what will happen in a negotiation.

7. **Be patient:** Don't get frustrated or upset if you can't get what you want. Remember that negotiations take time.

8. **Be willing to compromise:** Sometimes you have to be willing to give up something in order to get something else. If you can't find anything that both parties are willing to compromise on, then it might not be the best time to make the deal.

9. **Know when to walk away:** If you've tried everything and you're still unable to reach a deal, then it might be time to walk away.

10. **Don't be afraid to say no:** Don't let yourself get stuck in a negotiation because you're afraid to say no. You might think that you're giving something away by saying no, but

in the end, it will only benefit you.

I agree that the first three steps are most important. I also agree that you need to be clear on what you're offering and what you're getting in return. The fourth step is the key to the whole negotiation process. I think that if you can be clear on what you're offering and what you're getting, then the other party should be able to understand why you want what you want and why they should agree with you. The fifth step is one of the most important steps in the entire negotiation process. If you know what you want, you need to be clear about what you're offering. If you don't have a plan B, C, D, and E, then you're not being clear about what you're offering.

If you know what you want, but you aren't clear about what you're offering, then the other party might get frustrated because he or she isn't sure what you're getting. This can lead to confusion, which can lead to tension, which can lead to an impasse.

To avoid being trapped in a negotiation, it is crucial to have a vision and a plan. The better you understand what you want, the more likely you are to be able to communicate it to the other party.

How to Start & End a Negotiation

In negotiation, there is a lot more that goes on between the two parties than just money. *While the financial value of a deal may be the main focus, you have to look at the emotional value, the perceived value, and the social value of the deal.* This is especially true for entrepreneurs who are negotiating with their customers, as they must consider the perceived value of their brand. This can be especially important when you're trying to sell your products or services to the general public.

What does this mean? It means you're going to need to do some homework before starting a negotiation. If you want to know what's going on in your negotiations, you need to figure out what your goal is. Are you trying to make money or are you trying to prove that you can succeed at being an entrepreneur?

Don't get too far ahead of yourself. If you're stuck at a negotiating table, you've got to start with what you want. *"It sounds simple enough, but it's really easy to forget this,"* says Sam. *"You've got to think about what you want first."* It doesn't matter how many people are in the room with you if you don't know what you want. *"The trick is to say 'this' and make sure the other person gets the message."* After that, you should think about what the other person wants and decide if you want to help or hinder that person.

How to start and end a negotiation is pretty simple, and most of us know what to do. But not all negotiations are the same. Most business people negotiate the price of a product or service, but we often negotiate with our spouses, our children, or even our boss. Sometimes, we may need to convince someone of something we don't necessarily want. We may want something from them that they don't want to give us. Negotiating is a skill we use every day, but we don't always know how to get the results we want.

Negotiating requires two people: *a buyer and a seller.* You may find it hard to accept, but if you've ever been involved in a negotiation, you know that the key to success is not necessarily being able to convince your opponent of anything—it's understanding what they want, and then working backward to figure out what you can offer them that they'll want. This means asking yourself: *What are my priorities? What am I trying to accomplish? What are they trying to accomplish?*

Once you've figured that out, you can start discussing how to reach those goals, and what the best possible outcomes might be. This is where the "pitch" comes in. The term has a variety of uses, including a strategy for winning an argument (which we'll get into later). But it can also refer to a sales pitch, or even a sales call. If you're selling yourself, it's a strategy for persuading someone that you are the right person for the job. The idea behind pitching is simple: you give the person you're trying to sell something that they want—or at least something that they think they want. You show them why you're the best option. This could be a product, service, or job opportunity. If you're in a business relationship, it's a way to convince your customer that they should continue doing business with you. It might sound like a lot of work, but the payoff is enormous—you'll be more likely to get the result you want, and the other person will be more willing to help you achieve it. To make the pitch more effective, you need to be clear about what you're offering. That means knowing exactly what you're selling, what the person you're pitching to wants, and how you can provide it. Before you begin, you should know what you're selling. What are your goals? How will you reach them? What is the best way for them to get what they want?

If you're trying to persuade a customer to buy something, you'll need to be clear about your needs. *Are they looking for something that you can provide? Is there an opportunity for them to do business with you?*

If you're trying to sell yourself, you need to be clear about what you're offering: *your skills, knowledge, expertise, reputation, etc.* Think about why someone would want to hire you. *What do they want to accomplish? What will they get out of hiring you? This isn't the time to focus on your weaknesses*—you need to highlight your strengths, as well as what makes you unique.

The Pitch

The basic structure of the pitch is pretty straightforward: you begin by saying what you're offering. You then explain why that is important to the person you're pitching to. Finally, you finish with an ask.

Here are a few examples of pitches for different situations:

The Pitch: A job opportunity

The Buyer: I'm looking for a position in the marketing department. I have some experience in marketing, and I think I can bring a lot to the team.

Why should I hire you?

You: I've had success in marketing in the past. I've worked for companies like Microsoft and IBM, and I know what it takes to run a successful campaign. I'm looking to work in a fast-paced environment where I can help drive results. I can help you create a strong strategy, and help you deliver on your promises.

What would make you interested in me?

The Pitch: A customer relationship

The Buyer: We're doing business with someone else, but we're unhappy with how they're treating us.

Why should we continue doing business with you?

You: We've been working with another company for years. I think you'll be pleased with my work. I'm going to work hard to make sure our relationship continues to grow.

What are you looking for?

The Pitch: A product or service

The Buyer: We want to find a new way to manage our team. I've been looking at a lot of different tools, and I think you have a good product.

Why should I use your service? You: I've worked with other companies that offer similar services, and I'm impressed with how they do things. I can help you improve your product and your services. You'll get the best support from me, and I can help you grow your business.

What do you need to know?

The Pitch: A business relationship

The Buyer: I'm looking for someone to help me grow my business. I want to hire someone who is an expert in their field, and who has experience running a company.

What would make you interested in working for me? You: I've been a consultant for a few years. I know what it takes to be successful in business, and I know how to help you grow. I can provide the skills and expertise you need to make your company profitable.

Considering the examples above, now you have a clear idea of what you're offering, it's time to talk about why that is important to the person you're trying to sell to. You want to show them that you have something they want, or need. If you're selling a product or service, you want to convince them that they want the product or service that you're offering. You need to be clear about why they should buy from you instead of someone else—you need to be able to demonstrate that you're better than the competition. The way to do this is to give reasons why the other person should buy from you. You want to show how your product, service, or expertise is better than anything else available.

For example, if you're selling a product, you might say: *Your product is better than theirs because it's easier to use. Your product is better than theirs because it has fewer bugs. Your product is better than theirs because it has more features. Your product is better than theirs because it's more durable. Your product is better than theirs because it's cheaper, etc.*

A key skill for anyone who wants to negotiate is knowing how to start and end a negotiation. The key is to understand the value of an offer versus the value of your counteroffer. By comparing these two numbers, you'll be able to figure out if you're getting a good deal.

Chapter 4

The Best Strategies to Persuade Others

The best strategies to persuade others include personalizing the message, using emotional language, and keeping them engaged. It can be tempting to use the same strategies over and over again when trying to persuade someone. However, because humans are susceptible to boredom, you may need to vary your approach to keep people interested.

Personalizing the Message: When you're attempting to persuade others, it's important to think about how they'll perceive what you're saying. One of the best ways to do this is by making sure that you're addressing the individual, rather than a general audience. For example, if you're trying to persuade your friend to go to a party, you might say, "Hey, I know you have plans with your friends, but I really want you to come with me to this party. You'll have a great time!"

If you're trying to persuade someone to buy something from you, you might say, "Hey, I saw this cool new shirt at the mall today, and I think you'd like it. Let me know if you're interested."

Emotional Language: In addition to personalizing the message, you should also try to use emotional language. This can help you connect better with the person you're trying to persuade. For example, if you're trying to convince a friend to go to a party, you might say, "I know it sounds like I'm asking you to do something crazy, but I really want you to go to this party with me. It's going to be so much fun!"

Keeping Them Engaged: Even though you're trying to persuade someone, you should always keep them engaged. This means that you should ask open-ended questions and make sure that they understand what you're saying. In addition, you should keep them thinking about what you're saying. For example, if you're trying to persuade a friend to go to a party, you might say, "Hey, I really want you to come to this party. You're going to have a great time. What do you say?" If you're trying to persuade someone to buy something from you, you might say, "Hey, I saw this cool new shirt at the mall today, and I think you'd like it. Let me know if you're interested." It can be tempting to use the same strategies over and over again when trying to persuade others.

However, because humans are susceptible to boredom, you may need to vary your approach to keep people interested.

If you can't get your point across to others quickly and simply, you'll always struggle to persuade them. For this reason, it's important to learn to identify the basic strategies and techniques for effectively persuading others. They include the following:

1. **Persuade by building credibility, then authority:** In other words, people are persuaded most effectively by those they trust, rather than those who present themselves as authorities. By building a relationship with someone over time, you can establish that trust.

2. **Persuade by using credibility to sell authority:** Once you build credibility, you can then sell authority to make a sale. This is an effective technique because it puts the responsibility back on the customer to make a decision based on their evaluation of your advice.

3. **Persuade by showing empathy:** People are influenced

most by those who appear to understand their feelings, needs, and desires. You'll likely persuade others more effectively if you empathize with them.

4. **Persuade by using emotion to sell logic:** People are more likely to buy what they want, need, or fear. To persuade others, you must tap into these emotions and use them as leverage to get your message across.

5. **Persuade by asking questions:** The best way to persuade is to ask questions. By doing so, you're likely to get a better understanding of the person's situation. From there, you can develop a plan of action that addresses his or her concerns.

6. **Persuade by using social proof:** People are persuaded more easily when they see that others are doing it, and they're less likely to question the validity of the practice. For example, if you're talking about a new product, showing people how successful other people are using it will likely lead them to accept it.

7. **Persuade by using scarcity:** When you talk about something, be sure to include the "but" in your message. This shows that what you're offering is limited in some way. For example, when you tell someone that your new

product is the best, you can add, *"But we have only 50 of them left!"*

8. **Persuade by using scarcity to sell authority:** If you can point out a downside to something, you can then sell authority by saying, *"And that's why I'm recommending you do X instead."*

9. **Persuade by using scarcity to sell logic:** Once you've shown that what you're offering has a downside, it's time to point out all of the benefits of your product or service. By doing so, you'll make it clear how much better it is than what your customer is currently using, or how you can solve his or her problem better than your competitor.

10. **Persuade by using scarcity to sell emotion:** People are more likely to buy something when they see that others want it and are willing to pay more for it. For example, when you talk about a new product, you can show people how successful other people are using it by pointing out that it's been featured in magazines and on television.

How to Listen and Make Others Feel Comfortable

Listening and making others feel comfortable are two of

the most important aspects of being a good leader. Listening allows your employees to share what's going on in their lives or at work. Listening enables them to build trust and rapport, which is important for any relationship. This is why it's essential to be an open listener when interviewing potential new hires. Making others feel comfortable is equally important because it allows them to share what's bothering them or what they don't like about their jobs.

When you make others feel comfortable, you're showing them that you care about their well-being and that you respect them. The key to listening and making others feel comfortable is being able to understand what they're saying and why they're saying it. You need to be able to read between the lines, understand what they mean, and use that information to help them solve problems. <u>Being able to read people is the most important skill you can learn. If you can't read people, you won't be able to lead effectively.</u> It's difficult to get people to work with you if they don't think you can be trusted. And, you won't be able to help them solve problems if you can't understand what they mean.

As a leader, you should always be willing to learn more about your employees and what they're feeling. You should never assume that you know what they're thinking or that they're comfortable talking to you about it.

There are two key elements of listening and making others feel comfortable.

The first is to listen with your ears. You should be willing to listen and hear what others are saying. If you want to lead effectively, you need to listen. It's one of the most important skills you can develop.

The second element is to listen with your eyes. You should be able to see when people are not comfortable and give them the space and time they need to express themselves. This is a critical skill for any leader because people won't open up to you if you don't make them feel comfortable. They may say things they don't mean or tell you what you want to hear.

Listening is the basis for every relationship. Whether it's a conversation with a friend, a business relationship, or a personal one, we all need to learn how to listen. Listening is one of the best ways to connect to others and get to know them.

Listening is a simple skill. All you have to do is *pay*

attention. To be clear, listening doesn't mean nodding your head or saying *"I understand"*; it means actively listening and actively seeking to understand. If a colleague comes into your office, say, "Hey, what's up? How are you? I'm happy to see you!" If you're having a conversation with someone and it seems like they're telling you something, stop talking for a moment and let them finish. You'll be amazed at how quickly they'll feel comfortable and will probably continue to share the rest of what they had to say.

In your life as a leader, it's easy to take on the role of a listener. You assume that other people are listening and you assume that they're waiting for you to say something or to ask questions before they'll speak up. This is a dangerous assumption because the reality is that no one is waiting for you to speak. The truth is, the people in your life don't care if you have anything to say. They care about themselves. They care about their own needs and desires. And if you're not careful, you're going to end up doing exactly what they want you to do: talking. If you're not careful, you're going to make them feel good and feel important. You're going to talk over them. You're going to interrupt them. You're going to try to give them advice. You're going to make them feel like they're the only person in the room. You're going to tell them what you think they should be doing instead of what they're actually doing. It's not that you're a bad leader. It's that you're a good listener. How do we become better listeners? It's a lot easier than you might think.

When you're listening, you're not only listening to what your people are saying, but you're also listening to how they're saying it. You're paying attention to their tone and their volume. You're trying to figure out if they're being honest or if they're just talking to impress you. You're trying to figure out if they're angry or if they're sad or if they're just tired. You're trying to understand if they're frustrated or if they're relieved. You're trying to figure out if they're excited or if they're discouraged. You're trying to figure out if they're happy or if they're confused. And the truth is, none of those things matter. None of those things are even relevant. You don't care about their tone or their volume. You don't care if they're angry, sad, tired, frustrated, discouraged, excited, or confused.

The only thing that matters is what they're saying. That's why listening is so important. When you're not listening, you're actually listening to something else. You're listening to your own thoughts and feelings. You're listening to your own desires and needs. And you're listening to the way that your mind and your emotions are telling you that you want things to go. When you're not listening, you're not really listening to your people at all. You're listening to the things that you're telling yourself about them. So here's the thing, when you're not listening to your people, it's because you're trying to listen to your own thoughts and feelings. That's how you end up being unkind or even rude to them. That's how you end up feeling superior to them. That's how you end up feeling like you know better than they do.

Asking questions can help listeners better understand the speaker, and by asking follow-up questions, listeners can also better understand their own thoughts and feelings. Here are some ways to do this:

Start your question with a word or phrase that makes you feel comfortable, such as *"Do you...?"* or *"So how did you...?"* This shows your respect for the other person, and it helps them feel more comfortable sharing. It may also help if you ask in a way that gives the other person control over whether they want to answer.

For example, instead of saying *"How do you feel about...?"* say, *"Do you think...?"* or *"What do you think...?"*

Ask open-ended questions that encourage the other person to elaborate on their feelings. For example, say, *"Can you tell me more about what's going on with you right now?"* or *"Can you tell me more about why you feel like that?"*

Don't assume that the other person knows what you're talking about, and don't interrupt them until they have finished speaking. Ask *"Is that all?"* or *"Do you need more time?"* before you start asking questions. If you're having trouble understanding what someone is saying, ask for clarification. Say *"I didn't quite understand what you said,"* or *"Can you explain that again?"* If the other person doesn't clarify, you can say *"Okay"* or *"Go ahead"* to get them to keep talking. If the other person is being difficult, try using a different tone of voice.

For example, if the other person is angry or upset, use a softer, more calm voice. If the other person is defensive, use a louder, firmer voice. Try to understand why the other person might be feeling a certain way.

It's important to show respect and kindness towards others. You should never speak ill of someone or insult them in any way. You should also avoid sarcasm, and only say things that are true. Don't make fun of someone, and don't laugh at their situation. If you don't agree with someone, don't argue or discuss it with them. Instead, look for other ways to resolve the issue. Don't be afraid to ask for help. It's okay to ask for help from family members or friends who have more experience than you do. Remember, you're not alone! There are lots of people out there who can help. If you can't figure out what to say or how to react, remember these tips:

Try to stay calm: This will help you think clearly and make sure you're not saying something that you'll regret later.

Don't let fear take control of your emotions: Fear can cause you to act without thinking. You need to use your head, not your heart. You need to make decisions based on logic and reason, not feelings.

Don't argue with someone who is upset or angry: This

will only make them feel worse. Instead, try to understand their point of view. If you're having trouble figuring out what to say, don't say anything. You may end up saying something that you'll regret later. Just wait until you feel more comfortable.

It's okay to ask for help: It's okay to ask for help from family members or friends who have more experience than you do. Remember, you're not alone! There are lots of people out there who can help.

Most people like to feel valued and appreciated. The art of listening is the ability to pay attention to and understand what another person is saying, without interrupting. By paying attention, you show your appreciation and value to the speaker and are able to offer your input. This shows that you care about what they're saying and want to be involved. It also allows you to be part of the conversation, making it a win-win situation.

You can say "thank you" at any time during the conversation to acknowledge someone's thoughts or feelings. However, if you use this technique every time someone has something to say, they might think that you are being rude and start ignoring you. If you don't like the way someone is talking to you, you have two options.

First, you can simply let them know how you feel.

Second, you can express your concerns by saying something like, *"I'm not sure I understand what you're saying. Can you explain that?"*

If you want to make someone feel valued and appreciated, ask them questions about their thoughts and feelings. When you do this, they feel important and are more likely to open up. You can also say, *"I'm glad to hear that."* or *"That's interesting."* People who feel appreciated and valued enjoy sharing their thoughts and feelings.

When it comes to listening, a lot of people believe that you can tell a lot about a person by the way he or she talks. But that doesn't necessarily mean that this person is talking just to hear his or her own voice. Instead, this could just be a way to feel comfortable and accepted. People who talk a lot may just be trying to keep others calm or engaged. On the other hand, people who listen a lot might just be trying to understand what someone is saying.

You have probably heard of someone who is always trying to make sure that everyone else is okay. When someone is always talking, it can sometimes make it hard for others to get a word in. This is why, at times, you might find yourself asking for permission before speaking up. You don't want to be the one that makes people feel bad. There are a lot of different types of people who are good listeners. Some of these people are always trying to help. They are willing to listen to anyone who needs to talk. Other people are always listening to themselves. They aren't as interested in what others are saying, but they are definitely listening to their own thoughts. We all have different ways of making sure that we get what we need out of life. A lot of people are very goal-oriented. These people will work hard to achieve their goals. However, some people are more concerned with the journey. They are more focused on the experiences that they can gain along the way.

It is important to understand that not everyone is meant to be an extrovert or an introvert. Everyone has a unique set of skills and talents. Some people are good at being alone while other people need to be around people. If you are an introvert, you may find yourself feeling a little nervous when you go to a party. You may feel uncomfortable speaking up.

However, if you are an extrovert, you might find yourself being more comfortable when you are surrounded by a large crowd. You might feel more confident when you know that there is someone else to talk to. We all have different ways of making sure that we get what we need out of life. This can be difficult for people who are unsure of what type of personality they have. It can be hard to figure out who you are without someone else to help you. When you listen to others, your brain doesn't have to process all of the words being spoken. Instead, <u>you take in the tone of voice, volume, intonation, and facial expression of the speaker and react to it.</u> This is a very human response. We tend to avoid someone who's speaking loudly and interrupting us because they're making us uncomfortable.

How to Win Arguments and Debates

An argument is a statement or opinion designed to persuade the audience to change its position, while a debate is an extended exchange of opinions in which both parties make their points. They are persuasive in that they are designed to lead someone to a particular conclusion.

However, in a debate, there's no winner and no loser. Both parties must accept the final outcome. To win an argument, you must prove to the other side that they are wrong. A debate is the opposite; you don't want to win, you want to prove your opponent wrong. And that requires that you prove yourself right.

The basic premise of an argument is that two or more sides of an issue can be brought together to form a single point of view. A good argument has something for everyone. There's no single correct way to argue, but there is a framework for structuring arguments and making sure they are persuasive.

The framework we'll review is called *the four-step model of argument.*

Why should we learn to argue?

Arguments are often used in the business world, but they're also important in everyday life. Arguing is one of the most basic ways of resolving conflict. Whether you're having a disagreement with your spouse or boss, or you're trying to convince your friend to do something, the process is the same. In fact, the same framework can be applied to a variety of different situations, from academic debates to arguments about politics to arguments about what to watch on TV.

When you're arguing, there are two ways to win: _prove your opponent wrong, or prove that you're right._

You need to be prepared to defend your position and explain why it's better than the other side's. You need to make sure that your points are well-reasoned and that you present them in a way that makes sense. When you argue, you're putting yourself out there. If you argue well, you're showing that you have confidence in your own point of view and are willing to stand up for it.

A **_persuasive argument_** doesn't necessarily mean that you've convinced your audience to agree with you. _Persuasive arguments_ are designed to change people's minds, but they don't have to be winning arguments. In fact, most arguments aren't. A good argument will include both sides of an issue, but it won't necessarily have to be a winner. If you can use the framework of a persuasive argument to convince someone to agree with you, then you've won. If you can't, then you haven't won, but you still managed to argue well. The four-step model of argument is designed to help you do that.

The Four-step Model of an Argument

Let's look at the four-step model of argument in more detail.

Step 1: Framing:- The first step in any argument is to frame your topic in a way that makes sense to your audience. What do you want them to think about? Let's say you want them to think about a particular policy proposal. You might begin by asking a question: *"What are the benefits of this policy?"* By framing the question this way, you're giving your audience a reason to agree with your point of view. Your audience might have their own ideas about the benefits of the policy, so you need to be clear about what you mean when you ask, *"What are the benefits?"*

For example, you could ask, *"What are the positive effects of this policy?"* This would be a more specific way of framing the question, but it might not give your audience all the information they need to agree with you. Framing is a very important part of any argument because it helps you get your message across. If you don't understand how your audience thinks, you won't be able to persuade them.

You need to know who they are and what they care about before you can argue effectively.

Step 2: The first premise:- In step two, you need to make your first point of view clear. What is the first point of view that you're going to argue for? In the previous example, you might say that the benefits of the policy outweigh the risks. The first premise is where you lay the groundwork for your argument. It's also called <u>the "*premise*" of your argument</u>, or the <u>"*premise*"</u> for short. The premise of an argument is the most important part, because it lays out the basis of the argument. If you're not sure what the premise is, you can always ask your audience for help. *"What do you think the premise of this argument is?"* When you frame your argument in terms of a premise, it makes it easier for your audience to follow your argument. They know exactly where they are in the process of convincing you.

Step 3: The conclusion:- In step three, you need to make sure that your audience understands what you want them to do. What should they do? What do you want them to agree with you about? In the example above, you might say that the benefits of the policy outweigh the risks. This might be your conclusion, or it might be a summary of the first point you made. Either way, your conclusion is the end result of your argument. It's what you want your audience to agree with you about.

Step 4: The second premise: In step four, you need to make your second point of view clear. What is the second point of view that you're going to argue for? In the previous example, you might say that the benefits of the policy outweigh the risks, but you could also say that the policy is worth the risk. The second premise is where you restate your first point of view. If you're arguing against someone else's point of view, then you need to restate the first point of view in your own words. You're trying to get your audience to agree with you, so you need to give them reasons why they should do so. You're not trying to convince them to change their mind; you're trying to persuade them to agree with you. When you restate the first point of view, it gives your audience a chance to understand your point of view more clearly. It also lets them know that you have a reason for your second point of view.

The *four-step model* is a great framework for structuring arguments and making sure that they're persuasive. There are four steps, and each one builds on the one before it. When you follow the four-step model, you're taking the first step in an argument, but you're also building on the last step of the argument. It's like building a house: The foundation of the house is laid first, but the roof goes on top of it. Each step has a purpose, so you can't skip any of them. It's like a dance: If you skip a step, you'll never get to the end of the dance.

If you're in a debate or argument, don't fall into the trap of arguing for your side or trying to win the argument, but rather, simply listen and absorb your opponent's points. You can learn a lot about what they're saying just by listening. After all, you'll never be able to win an argument unless you understand it. And, if you truly understand the other side, you'll also be better prepared to argue your case effectively.

What separates the good debater from the bad is that the good debater makes a compelling case for his or her argument, but the bad debater tries to win by making the case against the other side appear weak.

In addition to this, the debater who wins the argument is perceived as intelligent, confident, and likable. So how do you win arguments and debates? One simple strategy is to begin with a strong position.

By starting from a strong position, you will always be viewed as more credible and sounder than your opponent. Once you have made your point clear, you need to be careful not to fall into the trap of becoming combative, defensive, and aggressive towards your opponent.

If you want to win an argument or debate, you have to put the other person in an emotional state of wanting to be right. To do that, you need to be right first. People are more likely to agree with your position if you're arguing for a position they already agree with. And if you want to win an argument or debate, you need to understand the psychological impact of the words you choose. This is why so many people lose debates and arguments because they don't listen to the other side.

Chapter 5

How to Work with Different Personalities and Personality Types

Each of us has a unique personality that is shaped by our experiences and environment. This makes us unique. So when you want to work with someone, it's important to understand that person's personality and your own in order to better work together.

According to Wikipedia, the five major personality types are *extrovert, introvert, empathizer, controller, and challenger.* Each of these personality types responds differently to the same stimuli. Understanding a person's personality type can help you better connect with that person, work with them, and manage them.

An Extrovert's Personality

Extroverts tend to be more outgoing and talkative than introverts. Extroverts are usually the ones that make most of the first impression. They are often seen as enthusiastic and gregarious, and they enjoy being in the center of attention. Extroverts usually have high energy levels and enjoy socializing with others. They are also often perceived as dynamic, creative, fun, and enthusiastic. Extroverts are not usually introspective or quiet; they are constantly seeking new ideas, new challenges, and new experiences. Because extroverts are social beings, they are usually good at dealing with other people. They also tend to enjoy working in groups and making connections with many people.

Extroverts are usually seen as confident and charismatic. They tend to be assertive and outgoing, and they tend to take charge. Extroverts are usually very energetic and enthusiastic. They also tend to be optimistic and enthusiastic. They are very goal-oriented and often set very high goals for themselves. Extroverts enjoy working in teams, and they tend to be very task-oriented. They like to be the leader, and they often take charge.

A Controller's Personality

Controllers tend to be more reserved and aloof than extroverts. Controllers tend to be the ones who stay in the background and keep their thoughts to themselves. Controllers are usually quiet, cautious, and wary of others.

They are usually very private, secretive, and guarded. Controllers usually have low self-esteem, and they tend to be sensitive and fearful of rejection. They tend to avoid conflict and are often very selective about how they deal with people. Controllers are usually seen as serious, dignified, and responsible. They are usually very disciplined and organized. Controllers enjoy working alone and tend to be efficient and organized. They are usually very private, reserved, and guarded. Controllers tend to be reserved, cautious, and wary of others.

An Introvert's Personality

Introverts tend to be more reserved than extroverts. Introverts tend to be very reserved, quiet, and shy. They are usually very private and secretive. Introverts usually have low self-esteem, and they tend to be sensitive and fearful of rejection. Introverts usually have low energy levels, and they tend to avoid socializing and being the center of attention. Introverts are usually seen as shy, reserved, and quiet.

However, they can be extremely intelligent. The following are some examples of introverts: Mark Twain, Albert

Einstein, Steve Jobs, Jane Austen, Albert Camus, Charles Dickens, George Bernard, Shaw Leonardo, etc.

An Empathizer's Personality

Empathizers are usually seen as very sympathetic, kind, sensitive, caring, and understanding. They are usually good listeners and tend to care about other people's feelings. They are usually perceived as empathetic and compassionate. They usually have high self-esteem and tend to be optimistic and enthusiastic.

In contrast, non-empathizers are usually seen as cold, indifferent, insensitive, uncaring, and unsympathetic. They don't usually like to hear others talk about their problems or feel sorry for them. They rarely listen to what other people say and often appear bored and uninterested. They may be perceived as selfish, insensitive, and uncaring. Empathizers tend to get along better with people, and non-empathizers tend to get along better with things. Empathizers usually have strong feelings about people. They tend to be very sympathetic and caring toward others. They may have a hard time expressing themselves or expressing their feelings.

A Challenger's Personality

Challengers are usually seen as very assertive and aggressive. They are usually seen as ambitious, goal-oriented, and competitive. They are usually very outgoing, dynamic, and assertive. Challengers usually have high energy levels, and they tend to be very energetic and enthusiastic. They usually have high self-esteem and tend to be very goal-oriented.

Challengers are usually quite independent and do not like being told what to do or how to behave. They can be bossy and demanding at times, but when they get a task accomplished they are very satisfied with themselves. Challengers are usually very confident, but they tend to be overconfident. This is probably because they have a lot of confidence in their own abilities and are not very good at dealing with failure. They can be stubborn and set in their ways, and this can sometimes be a problem when they are trying to learn something new.

People are all unique in their own special way, but that doesn't mean you can't work effectively with everyone.

How do you work with people who are different from you? People; who are high-achieving, driven, outgoing, and organized? How about people who are different in some way—maybe they're introverted or shy, maybe they're a perfectionist or procrastinate? Most of us interact with people all day long that don't align with our personality, but how can we work with them?

There are many ways to work with people who are different from you. If someone is high-achieving and successful, don't be afraid to ask them what they did to achieve success. If someone is shy and quiet, don't be afraid to ask them how they cope with their shyness. The key is to be genuine, open-minded, and respectful. Working with people who are different from you may take a little more effort than working with someone who shares your personality, but the rewards are worth it. If you want to become a more effective leader, working with people who are different from you can help you in so many ways.

Leadership is a mindset. It's not a position, title, or position of authority. You can lead someone in many different ways, but one of the most important things to remember is that leadership is an attitude. Leaders aren't born, they're made. When you're in a leadership role, you must work to develop a mindset that will allow you to succeed.

If you want to become an effective leader, here are some tips to work with people who are different from you:

Be genuine: Don't try to hide who you are when working with people who are different from you. Being genuine doesn't mean being fake or disingenuous, but it does mean being honest and authentic. Don't be afraid to share your own weaknesses and strengths, as well as those of your team members.

Be open-minded: When working with people who are different from you, don't assume that you know everything about them. You may not know what they do for a living or how long they've been in their role, so don't make assumptions about them. If you want to work effectively with someone, be curious about them. Ask questions and listen. Let them tell you their story, and learn from it.

Be respectful: Show respect to everyone you meet. Treat people with dignity and respect, and expect the same in return. If someone is rude or disrespectful, let them know that you find them to be inappropriate and that you don't appreciate their behavior. Respect is one of the most important things that you can demonstrate to people around you.

Work with your team members: Working with your team members will help you become an effective leader. It's important to work with your team members because you have a vested interest in their success. You may be able to provide some guidance and direction, but ultimately, your team members are responsible for their own success. When you work with them, they'll want to succeed as well, so it's important to develop a working relationship with them.

Being a good leader isn't about being perfect. It's about being committed to making your team better, more effective, and more efficient. The best leaders are authentic, open-minded, and respectful. They care about their team members, and they help them achieve success.

The 7 Types of People You Are Likely to Meet in a Negotiation

The three psychological principles that come into play in negotiations are ***expectancy, reciprocity,*** and ***consistency***. All three are important to know if you want to win a negotiation, and all three require knowing how to read people. The key to success in any negotiation, whether online or offline, is to recognize and understand the different types of people you may be dealing with.

There are two aspects of the self that you must consider: your own personality and how it affects others. It's true that "you" can't change what other people think, but you can influence how they view you and your intentions. This is particularly relevant when negotiating. Your ability to influence another person is based on the following:

When you're going to negotiate, you have to know the types of people you'll be negotiating with. And just as important, you have to know the psychological principles that apply in every negotiation. For example, people who are high in extraversion tend to be warm, friendly, and open. They like to talk about themselves. In contrast, introverts prefer to talk about their ideas and goals.

Because of their differences in personality, negotiations between these two types of people will differ. You can also recognize when you're dealing with a difficult personality type.

There is no such thing as a *"type"* when it comes to negotiation. But there are definitely certain personality traits that tend to be associated with each type, and you need to know which one you are in order to navigate any kind of negotiation effectively. So; whether you're negotiating a salary, a partnership, or something else, you need to know your personality type in order to make sure you're presenting yourself appropriately and communicating with the person you're negotiating with in a way that will help you both reach a successful outcome. I'm not talking about the kind of personality traits that can be measured by a personality test, such as the **Myers-Briggs Type Indicator** or the **NEO Personality Inventory (NEO PI-R)**. I'm talking about the general personality traits that make up your style and how they affect how you negotiate. When it comes to personality type, there are two major models: the **Big Five model** and the **Five Factor Model**. Each has its own strengths and weaknesses.

How to Avoid Being Bullied in the Process of Negotiation

Bullying is a common problem in the world of negotiation. Bullies tend to bully others by using a power structure that gives them a position of strength over others. They gain an advantage by leveraging their own resources, and force others into submission using threats. In negotiation, bullies are often persuasive and aggressive, but rarely negotiate with the other side. They'll typically try to win at all costs, which means making offers that are impossible for the other party to accept. When you're in a negotiation with someone who is trying to bully you, you want to avoid taking on the role of a bully yourself. This will only reinforce their position of power over you. Instead, play the role of the victim.

To be clear, I don't mean *"playing the victim"* as a way of getting out of having to negotiate. Rather, it's a strategy for how to negotiate effectively. If you know that your counterpart is a bully, use this strategy to ensure that you can walk away from the negotiation with an outcome that is beneficial for you.

Remember: The person with the most power in a negotiation is the one who can walk away. If you know someone who's being bullied, what should you do? Listen to their perspective. If you don't know what they're going through, ask questions. They may have been dealing with a bully for years and they may not want to tell you. But if you show that you care about them and are willing to listen, they will open up to you. Encourage them to get help from a professional.

Bullying is a common negotiating tactic used to get what you want. This often happens because one person doesn't feel comfortable or confident in negotiating. In those instances, the bully uses intimidation and pressure tactics to make the other person feel uncomfortable. These tactics include threats of loss of money, threats to harm someone's family, or even physical intimidation. It may seem like bullying is a one-way street, but it's actually a two-way street. The bully is always trying to push the other person's buttons. When you're the one being bullied, you can either give in to the bully's demands or you can stand up for yourself and negotiate your way out of the situation.

Negotiating Skills for Bullies

Bullies often try to use their negotiation skills to intimidate you into doing what they want. They may ask you to do things that are unreasonable or impossible for you to do. You may feel pressured to do things that will cause you to lose money or time. Bullies may also try to make you feel guilty about not agreeing with them. These tactics can be difficult to negotiate against because bullies know that most people will give in to pressure rather than risk the loss of something important to them. Bullies will often use the "I'm right" tactic to show how powerful they are and how much they're willing to do to get their way. This tactic makes them feel strong and important. If you try to negotiate with a bully, he may become angry or even violent. Bullies may attack you physically or verbally. They may threaten you with physical violence. Bullies may also be able to influence your friends and coworkers to back them up. Bullies are usually well organized, so they can use their power and knowledge to convince others that what they're doing is right. They may also try to convince others that you are the one who's wrong.

A bully, like most bullies, thrives on power. When you're negotiating with someone who's a bully, your best strategy is to avoid giving them any ground. It's not that you should be a bulldog; you just don't want to give the bully an inch, because you could easily lose the whole battle. Bullies use all kinds of tactics to try and take the high road, like making themselves seem bigger or intimidating you with threats, but they really are just bullies and they're playing dirty.

If you can figure out how to deal with a bully without giving them any power, you'll win every time. I've been bullied, and I know how it feels. I'm a grown-ass man who was once bullied as a kid, so I can tell you that it sucks. It's not fun. And when you realize that your bully is the only one in control, you have to think twice about how to respond. But if you can keep your cool and walk away from the situation without losing your dignity, you'll have no trouble winning. You can avoid being bullied in negotiations if you do two things.

First, **Know Your Strengths and Weaknesses:** To win in a negotiation, you need to know what your strengths and weaknesses are. You need to be aware of your weaknesses so you can avoid them when negotiating. A good way to figure out what your strengths and weaknesses are is to make a list of your achievements. If you're good at anything, you should be able to list several achievements. For example, if you're good at cooking, you might list *"cooks delicious meals for my family."*

Next, **be aware of your opponent's strengths and weaknesses**. Pay attention to their actions and words. If they're bullying you, you can see that by their words and actions. Ask yourself: Do they try to dominate the conversation? Do they try to get you to agree to unreasonable terms? Do they interrupt you often? If you see these signs, it means they are trying to bully you. Another thing you can do to avoid being bullied in a negotiation is to avoid giving them power over you.

Chapter 6

How to Become a Master Negotiator and Achieve Superior Results

The ability to negotiate, whether it be with your spouse, your boss, or another person, is something many people don't consider when they're entering into a new relationship or job. However, negotiating is critical for success in any situation, and the better you become at it, the more effective and successful you will be in your dealings with others. Negotiation involves influencing, persuasion, and getting someone else to agree with you. It also takes practice.

Why Should You Negotiate?

The ability to influence and persuade others is a key skill that can have many applications. Whether you want to get out of doing something you don't like, persuade someone to go along with your plan, or convince a friend to help you out, negotiation skills are a great asset to have in your repertoire. It's important to understand that negotiations aren't about winning or losing, but about achieving the best possible outcome.

When negotiating, your goal is to become a master negotiator. It's not always easy to understand why, but if you focus on becoming a master negotiator, you'll start to see the same tactics used by successful negotiators all around you. In fact, most negotiation experts agree that the only real difference between a great negotiator and a bad one is that great negotiators don't rely on tactics that aren't in line with the law of reciprocity. So, what are these tactics? Let's look at them.

The Law of Reciprocity: If you're negotiating with someone who has an emotional attachment to something he wants, you can use this law to your advantage. <u>The law of reciprocity says that you should offer something to the other person if he gives you something in return.</u> The best way to understand this law is to think about how you behave when buying a car or a house. If you ask for a discount on your car or home, you'll often be offered one in return. Why is this? The reason is that most people want to get things they need and deserve. So, they'll do anything it takes to get them. This applies to negotiations, too. If you offer a deal that your opponent can live with, he's more likely to accept it. You can use this law in two ways: by offering concessions in return for concessions you're asking for or by giving something to the other person in exchange for something you're asking for.

Now, let's talk about the first way. Imagine you're negotiating with your boss over a raise. If you ask for a raise and then agree to work on some projects that are not related to your position at the company, you may be able to get a significant raise. In return, you might agree to do some of the projects that are not directly related to your job. If you want to use this law, you need to make sure that what you're offering is something the other person wants and is willing to give up.

The first step in becoming a master negotiator is to stop selling yourself short. You have to start with a clear understanding of who you are and what you're worth. You need to know the value you bring to the table, and you need to understand how much you're willing to give up to make things happen. It's essential to make sure that your negotiating strategy supports your self-image. You also need to understand the mindset of those you're negotiating with. For example, if your job is to negotiate a salary increase, you can't be afraid to ask for more money. However, if your boss is a micromanager, your negotiating tactics may backfire. You might end up losing valuable time and making the situation worse. When you understand the real value you bring to a negotiation, you'll have a better idea of how to approach the negotiation process. The following questions will help you get a handle on the value you bring to the table: What do I bring to the table? What do I need to be successful in this negotiation? How much am I willing to lose if I don't succeed? What do I want to happen in the negotiation? How can I make that happen?

In negotiations, a master negotiator is one who is able to move others to a level of agreement faster than others, because he or she has mastered the art of negotiation. Master negotiators are able to build rapport very quickly, because they know how to take advantage of the other person's strengths while using their own strengths to leverage the other person's weaknesses. These skills include the ability to listen actively, understand and interpret non-verbal cues, and understand what drives the other person.

How to become a master negotiator

It takes time to develop your negotiation skills. The more you negotiate, the better you will get at it. Remember that if you want to learn from experience, you have to pay for it. When you are negotiating, be prepared to walk away from a deal. Negotiating is not about getting everything that you want. It is about getting what you need to get what you want. And it is never about being the winner or the loser, but rather the one who is satisfied. The art of negotiating involves being able to listen actively, understand and interpret non-verbal cues, and understanding what drives the other person.

How to make an impromptu negotiation work: When it comes to impromptu negotiations, your first instinct may be to give up. After all, impromptu negotiations can be quite challenging. But remember that your opponent is also trying to get what he wants. You can't just go in there with your mind already made up. To succeed at impromptu negotiations, you must keep your cool. If you feel like giving up, take a moment to think about why you are doing this.

Don't be afraid to ask for what you want: It's important to be clear about what you want and don't want. Don't be afraid to say "No." In fact, one of the best ways to make an impromptu negotiation work is to ask for what you want.

Be flexible: Impromptu negotiations are often stressful because of the uncertainty involved. It's important to be flexible in these situations. You need to be able to adapt your position if you realize that you're not getting the deal you wanted.

Be prepared: You should be prepared for any type of impromptu negotiation. This means that you should have the necessary information to make a successful decision, so that you can make the most informed choice possible. You should also have a plan of action that you can follow in case things don't go your way. Impromptu negotiations are often stressful because of the uncertainty involved.

The Top 10 Secrets of Masterful Negotiation

One of the best things you can do in business is learn how

to negotiate effectively. Negotiating is one of those skills that almost anyone can learn. While negotiating may not sound like a fun activity, it's something that nearly everyone does on a daily basis. So, if you haven't picked up some negotiation techniques yet, here are the top 10 secrets you need to know about how to get more out of the deals you make and the situations you find yourself in. Negotiating can be intimidating, but it doesn't have to be. In fact, negotiating is actually quite easy when you know the right moves to make. You just need to know what to do when you're in a position where you need to ask for more money or get something else from your employer. So, here are the top 10 negotiation secrets you need to know about how to get more out of the deals you make and the situations you find yourself in:

Secret # 1: <u>Don't be afraid to walk away</u> Don't just sit there and take whatever you're offered. If it doesn't meet your expectations, walk away. Walking away from a negotiation gives you three advantages. First, it shows that you don't accept less than what you want. Second, it puts an end to the negotiation. Third, walking away gives you the opportunity to start a new negotiation.

Secret # 2: Don't fall for the "I have a better offer" line Don't ever say, "I've got a better offer." If you're not going to accept your initial offer, say so and walk away. In other words, if you think you can get a better deal somewhere else, say, "I'm sorry, but I've already got a better deal somewhere else. " This will stop the negotiating process dead in its tracks.

Secret # 3: Don't be afraid to make offers. Don't ever sit there and say, "That's all I can afford." If you're really serious about getting more out of your negotiations, make an offer. Say, "I'll take this car for $1000 less than what you offered me if you give me an additional $100 in accessories. " The point here is that you should never accept less than what you want. If you do, it will become part of the negotiation.

Secret # 4: Don't let them walk away from you. It's very important to remember that the other side of a negotiation is not always a friend. They're not there to help you.

They're not there to be fair. They're not even there to make a deal. They're there to make a deal for themselves. Don't let them walk away from you. Do everything you can to get them to agree to your terms.

Secret # 5: <u>Know what you want and what you don't want.</u> Negotiations are not about getting things. Negotiations are about getting what you want. If you don't know what you want, then the only thing you can negotiate is what you don't want. So, when you're trying to negotiate, ask yourself, "What am I willing to accept? What am I willing to give up? What am I not willing to compromise on?"

Secret # 6: <u>Make sure you have something of value to offer.</u> First of all, you'll need to have something of value to offer if you want to be successful at negotiating. You need to know what it is that you have that others don't. The key is that you have something of value that someone else wants. Remember, it's not about giving and getting, it's about having something that someone else wants.

Secret # 7: <u>Always Ask For More.</u> The first thing that you should do when negotiating is to always ask for more money or more time. This is one of the most important things that you can learn when it comes to negotiating. If you don't ask for more, then you will never get more. If you aren't willing to ask for more, then you might as well just give up now because there is no way you are going to get what you want. So, the best thing that you can do is to always ask for more money and more time.

Secret # 8: <u>Know The Basics.</u> There are only a handful of things that you need to negotiate from the start. You don't need to spend hours negotiating a deal if you have a good idea of what you want and what the other person wants. For example, if you're buying something, it's important that you know the price you want to pay. You also want to know what you want from the seller so you can determine whether they're willing to meet your demands.

Secret # 9: <u>Know What To Say To Get More Money</u> If you want to negotiate for more money, it's important to understand exactly what you should say. In fact, you need to know what to say and when to say it in order to get what you want. For example, if you want a raise, you might need to let your boss know that you're willing to take a pay cut if they can give you a raise. That way, you're not giving up too much, but you're also not asking for too much.

Secret # 10: <u>Use the power of reciprocity.</u> This is a negotiating strategy that has been used for thousands of years. It's based on the idea that if someone gives you something, then you have to give them something back. For example, if your boss gives you a bonus, then you should give them some time off work. This is called "reciprocity" because you're giving and getting back. This is a powerful tool because it creates an emotional connection between you and the person you're negotiating with.

How to Negotiate when You're Under Pressure

Negotiations that begin with a sense of urgency often lead to an impasse. While the parties involved may not realize it, this is because their initial approach is fundamentally flawed. The way to negotiate successfully under pressure is to establish clear, measurable goals first and build toward them over time. The problem with the initial approach is that it often fails to recognize the reality of what the parties are trying to accomplish. As a result, the goal posts keep shifting. This creates the impression that the parties are on a collision course, which only serves to increase the urgency. But the fact is that they have no real disagreement over the ultimate goal. They just need to work out the details. A successful negotiation begins with the parties agreeing on the end goal. Once this has been accomplished, each party will then start to work on ways to achieve it. In addition to establishing the desired outcome, there are three other areas that must be addressed in order to ensure success:

1. the parties must understand their differences;

2. both parties must commit to doing what it takes to get to the agreed-upon goal; and

3. both parties must be willing to compromise.

The first step is for both parties to recognize their differences and understand them. The more closely they examine their differences, the better equipped they will be to overcome them.

Negotiating can be stressful and confusing for many people. But if you understand how to manage the stress and pressure of the negotiating process and use your best negotiating skills, you'll win the day. The key to negotiating successfully is to realize that you need to make sure you're being clear, concise and specific. Your tone, volume, gestures and facial expressions should all help you convey your message. Once you have the details of your negotiations laid out and agreed upon, you can proceed with confidence.

The first step in any negotiation is to define your goals. What do you want to achieve? In a business deal, what's your bottom line? Do you want to get a new product on the market or increase sales? Do you want to lower your costs or increase profits? If you don't know what your goals are, it can be difficult to determine what you want to achieve during the course of the negotiations. You'll need to think about these questions before you begin and decide how important they are to you.

If you're feeling pressured when negotiating, you should be thinking about whether you're in a position of strength. One thing to keep in mind is that your natural instinct might be to cave in to the other side's demand when you feel like you're in a bind. This is a very bad habit to fall into, and it's easy to tell if you're doing it because you're really worried about the outcome. Instead, take the time to think about whether you are truly in a bind, and consider if you have any alternatives. If you're able to come up with one, then you might be able to use that as leverage to make them back down on some of their demands.

The next thing to keep in mind is that you don't need to take things all the way to the end. You can walk away from the negotiations at any point if you feel like you've gotten everything you want. In fact, this is often a good idea if you feel like you're being taken advantage of. Make a list of all the pros and cons of your deal, and see if there are any better deals out there. There's always another option out there, and you might find that you get more money in some other way. If you have a friend or family member who can give you some advice, you might want to ask them for some input. They might have heard of an industry insider who has an even better deal, or they might have their own deal to offer. In any case, don't be afraid to look elsewhere.

There are three elements of negotiation that you should keep in mind:

First, don't assume that the other person is looking for the same thing you are. Second, always look to your opponent's needs. And third, understand the power of counter offers.

The last two elements may seem like common sense, but I've seen many people in negotiations make poor assumptions and take their opponents' needs for granted. This can lead to a negotiation that is all about your ego and your needs. Negotiating under pressure requires some humility. Pressure can sometimes cause us to lose our ability to think logically and make rational decisions. It can also cause us to feel as if we can't negotiate unless we're under extreme stress. This doesn't mean you can't negotiate effectively when you're stressed. However, there are ways that you can manage the situation and remain calm and cool while negotiating.

Remember, the goal of negotiation is to find a win-win solution. It's not to make yourself feel better or to win at someone else's expense. You need to keep in mind that the other party has their own agenda, too, and they may be thinking about their needs, as well as yours. The goal of negotiation is to achieve a win-win solution. You don't want to be negotiating under pressure because you're worried that you won't get your way. If you find yourself feeling nervous during a negotiation, it might be time to take a few deep breaths. If you feel like you can't breathe, then it's time to take a walk around the block or to step outside. Make sure that you have plenty of fresh air because negotiating under stress can be a bit overwhelming for some people. You should also try to avoid talking about stressful topics while you're negotiating.

The 5 Mindset Changes You Must Make to Succeed as a Negotiator

There are several ways to view negotiation. <u>One is as a game of chicken. A second perspective is that of a give and take relationship.</u> If you're willing to share more than you take, you'll usually get more than you give. <u>The third perspective is the win-win</u>. You win if you get what you need and the other person wins if you both get what you need. <u>And the fourth perspective is win-lose.</u> You win if you get what you want and the other person loses if they don't get what they want.

If you have an important negotiation to conduct, you should consider all four perspectives. Each perspective has its strengths and weaknesses. You should also consider how well each perspective will work in your particular situation. It's always best to know what you're up against before you make a deal. You can choose any combination of the four perspectives that work for you. For example, you might try to *win-win-lose, win-lose-lose, or lose-win-lose*. Or you may prefer to use only one perspective.

Whatever you do, you need to be aware of the consequences of your actions.

You must develop your mindset if you wish to negotiate successfully. Successful negotiators aren't born that way, but become that way through years of training. As in any profession, *negotiation is a learned skill*. But it's also a *mental skill*. Most people assume that successful negotiators are born that way. Not true. They become so by learning how to think differently from non-negotiators. Successful negotiators don't just think differently, they think differently in certain ways. That's why they have more success than non-negotiators. Negotiators can do this because they've developed the ability to think of negotiation as a means to an end. It's not just something they do to get something they want. It's a means to achieve a goal. When you start thinking about negotiating as a means to an end, you begin to change your mindset. You shift from thinking *"I want this. I'll go to any length to get it."* To thinking *"I need this to meet my goals. How can I get it?"* If you approach negotiations this way, you will be amazed at how much better they turn out. Negotiating as a means to an end is a different way of thinking. It's not a natural way of thinking for most people. But it's the only way to win consistently in negotiations.

In negotiation, mindset is everything. In fact, research suggests that your mind can either lead you to success or failure depending on how it frames things. Here are five of the most influential mindsets that you must adopt as you navigate the tricky world of negotiations.

Negotiation Mindset 1 - The Thinker: The thinker mindset means you are likely to make a decision based on what you think will happen. It's a riskier strategy than the optimist and the pessimist, but it is more likely to yield results. When you think, *"I have to negotiate with this person because they're too difficult to deal with,"* you will probably end up in a stalemate. When you think, "I have to negotiate with this person because they'll be able to help me get what I want," you are much more likely to get what you want. So the next time you are negotiating with someone, try to think about the outcome you want and see if you can start from there.

Negotiation Mindset 2 - The Optimist: Optimists are

known for their ability to see the glass as half-full. They tend to look at problems as opportunities. When you are optimistic, you are likely to be more flexible and less confrontational. This is the mindset that allows you to focus on solutions instead of just complaints. Negotiators who adopt this mindset tend to be more successful. If you are the optimist in a negotiation, you're probably wondering why your counterpart isn't behaving this way. If you're the optimist in a negotiation, you're probably wondering why your counterpart isn't behaving this way.

Negotiation Mindset 3 - The Realist: Realists tend to see things as they are. They focus on facts and data. They are likely to take things at face value. When you are realistic, you are more likely to take the high road and to be less emotionally driven. This is the mindset that helps you stay focused on your goal and not get sidetracked by other people's emotions or behavior. If you are the realist in a negotiation, you're probably wondering why your counterpart isn't behaving this way. The Realist Negotiator If you are the realist in a negotiation, you're probably wondering why your counterpart isn't behaving this way.

Negotiation Mindset 4 - The Resilient Negotiator: The Resilient Negotiator is able to bounce back from adversity. You're resilient when you can maintain your composure when facing difficulties. You will be the most successful negotiator if you can remain calm and collected during tense situations. If you are the optimist in a negotiation, you're probably wondering why your counterpart isn't behaving this way. Resilience is the ability to bounce back from adversity. You can't expect to succeed in your negotiations if you don't learn how to manage your emotions and your stress level. The Resilient Negotiator is able to bounce back from adversity. You're resilient when you can maintain your composure when facing difficulties. You will be the most successful negotiator if you can remain calm and collected during tense situations.

Negotiation Mindset 5 - The Reluctant Negotiator: The Reluctant Negotiator is hesitant to engage in the process.

This is not always a bad thing. Sometimes it's better to take a step back and analyze the situation. It can also be a sign that you need to improve your skills or negotiate with other people. If you are in a negotiation where you have more than one choice, and you have to make a decision, ask yourself, "Is this really the best option for me?" It is important to remember that if you don't like what you are offered, you don't have to accept it. It is also important to note that when you are negotiating with someone who has more power than you, you need to use your leverage.

Chapter 7
The 8 Most Common Pitfalls of Negotiation

When a negotiation starts, the odds are generally stacked against you. The person sitting across the table from you knows exactly what they're asking for, and they're aware of what you're willing to give. On the other hand, you don't know what you're looking for. You don't have any idea what kind of price range you're prepared to pay. You don't even know if the person sitting across from you is a good negotiator or not.

So; *how do you overcome that initial disadvantage?*

How can you make sure that you're in a position to succeed? The answer is that you need to be armed with at least four things:

- The ability to see what the other side is asking for.
- The ability to tell what you're willing to give.
- The ability to walk away if you don't like what

you're hearing.

- The ability to recognize a bad deal when you see it.

The first two are fairly easy to learn, and they apply to every negotiation. The third and fourth take a little more work. But once you've got those down, you'll be ready to get started on the really tough ones.

First of all, let's talk about the ability to see what the other side is asking for. In order to do that, you need to start by figuring out what you want. What is it that you want? Is it something that you absolutely have to have? Or is it something that you can live without? If it's the latter, then it's probably best to walk away. You don't want to waste your time on a negotiation if you don't really need what you're buying or selling.

A negotiation checklist can help you avoid the most common pitfalls and reduce the chances of losing your hard-earned deal. The most common pitfall of negotiation is failure to ask for the deal that you want, and failure to negotiate for the deal that you want. Both of these mistakes can lead to failure at the end of the day.

A negotiation checklist can help you avoid these mistakes and get what you want out of a negotiation. A negotiation checklist is a tool that helps you prepare for a negotiation and reduces the risk of making mistakes. When you are trying to get a good deal out of a negotiation, it can be easy to make mistakes and end up with a bad deal. There are many things to keep in mind when negotiating, but you need to take action to prevent some of the most common mistakes.

Negotiation is hard. When you're negotiating with another person, you're often faced with questions like: How am I supposed to negotiate with someone who's not interested in my proposal? Or, how should I negotiate with someone who's already offering me everything I'm asking for? It's not always easy to know what to do when it comes to negotiations.

There are several common pitfalls that can cause a negotiation to go wrong. Here are the top eight:

1. Negotiating too soon: If you're already at an impasse, it can be hard to tell if your negotiation is going to be successful or not. If the other party isn't willing to budge on any of their requests, you may feel like you've done all you can and it's time to move on. However, this is a common mistake that many people make when negotiating. You need to give yourself enough time to get to a point where you have a clear understanding of how much you can realistically expect from the other person. This will help you avoid being in a position where you feel like you're forced into making concessions that you don't want to make.

2. Negotiating too little: If you're always negotiating for more than you want to get, you may find that you end up with less than you expected. This is especially common when you're negotiating with someone who has more money, power, or resources than you do. In those cases, you need to make sure you negotiate for as much as you can, but only if you can realistically expect to get it. You should also make sure you negotiate for things that are important to you. You'll be able to avoid feeling like you didn't get enough if you have something you really wanted to get in the deal.

3. Negotiating in secret: As you may have guessed,

negotiating in secret is a bad idea. There are two main reasons why this is a bad idea: First of all, people don't tend to negotiate well if they know that the other person isn't going to reveal what they're offering. This is especially true if there's a possibility that they could change their mind and offer less later on. Second of all, it's not very effective. If the other party doesn't want to negotiate in public, then you can't really pressure them into it. You'll have to accept whatever they're willing to offer you.

4. You Don't Know What You Want: It sounds simple, but it's very common. A lot of times, people start negotiations without knowing exactly what they want or need. If you don't know what you want, then how can you negotiate with someone else about getting what you want? To solve this problem, first make sure you have all the information necessary to understand what you want. Then, come up with a list of things that you want and needs, along with a specific budget, timeline, and desired outcome.

5. You Negotiate For The Wrong Reasons: It's one thing to negotiate for the sake of negotiating. That's fine when you have an objective to gain or a specific goal to achieve. But if your only reason for negotiating is to make yourself feel better, then you're likely not going to get what you want. You should be negotiating because you genuinely want something and you're willing to work towards getting it.

6. You Should Know What You Want: Once you've got your list together, start thinking about what you want and why you want it. If you don't know why you want it, then you won't be able to negotiate effectively. So, think about why you want it, and keep coming back to that idea until you can clearly define what it is you want. Then, come up with a plan of action for getting what you want.

7. You Should Be Willing To Negotiate: This is where people get into trouble. Not preparing properly. Negotiating is an art that requires preparation. Before you sit down to talk to your boss about that raise or your friend about the house you're trying to buy, make sure you have all of your ducks lined up. Know exactly what you want and be prepared to back it up with facts and figures. If you don't know what you're asking for, chances are you won't get it. Thinking you'll be able to "just ask" for something. Asking is great.

8. Negotiating with a Negotiator: You've probably heard that you should never negotiate with a negotiator. But what if the other person has a point? If they're offering you something that seems fair, then they may be able to help you reach a more favorable deal. They might even make your job easier. For example, say that you and your boss are trying to figure out how much you should be paid. Your boss is offering you $30,000, while you're asking for $40,000. In this case, it might be a good idea to negotiate with your boss.

The 3 Most Important Questions to Ask Before Your First Negotiation

Negotiations are a tricky business for both parties involved. Negotiating successfully is one of the most critical skills to possess if you're going to be in business of any kind. You need to know how to get what you want and ensure that you get what you deserve. We all negotiate. Whether it's our salary, a raise or a promotion, we are constantly negotiating. The best negotiators know this and they learn how to do it. If you're not good at it, it could cost you your job, or worse. The best way to learn how to negotiate is to watch other people negotiate. Watch them negotiate their way to success and you can learn from them. When you understand how they do it, you can use that information to negotiate your way to the top. Negotiating is all about knowing your audience. If you don't know who you are negotiating with, then you can't get what you want.

Negotiation is a difficult skill to master. It takes years of practice to perfect. Once you have mastered the art of negotiation, you will never have to worry about losing again. You may have to negotiate with people in different positions, but you will be able to win every time. The most important thing to remember when negotiating is that if you don't like the answer, you can always walk away. That means you have no need to go into negotiations feeling angry or frustrated. Anger and frustration are negative emotions that only bring you more problems.

Negotiation is a necessary part of business. It's an

opportunity to work together towards common goals and to overcome challenges. It's also a chance to show who you are as a human being. As such, it's a process full of emotion and tension. It's important to understand the negotiation process, because if you don't, you may end up with a bad deal and end up regretting it. Here are three questions to ask before the first negotiation, to help make sure you're negotiating in the best interest of both parties.

Question 1: *How Will This Negotiation Impact Your Relationship?* Negotiation is a two-way street. You're going to have to give something up if you want something else. So; how will this negotiation impact your relationship? How will it affect the future of your relationship? If you don't understand this, you may end up making a bad deal that will negatively impact your relationship.

Question 2: *What Will This Negotiation Mean To Me?* This one is really important. You have to ask yourself, what does this mean to me? Will I lose a job? Will I get fired? Will I be able to keep my home? Will I have to move in with my parents? These are all valid questions to ask when considering a potential negotiation.

Question 3: *How Am I Going To Approach This Negotiation?* This is one of the most important questions you should ask yourself before you start talking to the other person. What are you going to do to make sure this negotiation goes well? Are you going to be calm and collected?

The answers to these questions will help you formulate a win-win strategy. For example, if you want to get your boss to agree to give you a raise, start with: "Mr. Jones, I'm going to do everything I can to help our company grow and prosper. But to do that, I need to be compensated fairly for my efforts.

What's Your Bottom Line?

When negotiating, you should always start by asking yourself what your bottom line is. What will you be willing to do or give up if you can't reach an agreement? What are your terms? You need to be clear about your bottom line before you even start negotiating. The more clearly defined your bottom line is, the better you'll be able to understand what needs to be done in order to reach an agreement. As a general rule, your bottom line should be realistic and achievable.

If your bottom line isn't realistic or achievable, it's time to think about your negotiating strategy. I have worked with many clients over the years who were successful in their negotiations because they kept their bottom line realistic and achievable. I have also seen clients who failed at negotiations because they didn't know their bottom line and because they allowed unrealistic goals to get in the way of reaching an agreement. So what's your bottom line? It should be realistic and achievable. If you don't have a bottom line, then you probably don't know what you want.

6 Ways to Make a Negotiation Winnable

The more you know about negotiation, the better equipped you'll be to make the sale and walk away with a win. But, there's one question that really gets me every time I teach this class: *"Why should I negotiate?"* This is a great question. Because most of us don't negotiate on a regular basis, we forget how valuable it is. And because we often get so caught up in our own business, we sometimes forget about the value of negotiating for others. If you're a business owner, you should be asking yourself this question all the time. You may have already negotiated deals with your customers or suppliers. But do you really know what you've got in those deals? What if you could find out? What would that mean to your business?

I had the opportunity to speak recently at the Atlanta Business Chronicle annual conference. I was asked to talk about negotiation. It was a very different experience for me than speaking in front of an audience. My job was to teach my audience about negotiation and give them some tips on how to get more of what they want. At the same time, I was getting to hear about the struggles of other speakers who were sharing their stories of failure. In a world where everyone seems to be failing, it is easy to feel like you're on the outside looking in. The truth is, we all fail sometimes. It's how we recover from that failure that can make or break our business. The key to negotiating successfully is to be able to take responsibility for your own success. This means understanding the reasons why you are failing so you can learn from your mistakes. If you can do that, you'll be able to get more out of your next negotiation.

The Problem: Negotiation is not something most people enjoy. Most people hate it. They think of it as a way to lose. I hate it because I think it's a way to win. But I love to negotiate, and it has been my job to teach others how to negotiate as well. That means teaching them how to get more of what they want in their business or life. This is one of the biggest challenges I face in teaching people how to negotiate. When it comes to a negotiation, one thing is clear: if both parties are willing to listen and willing to compromise, it can lead to a win-win situation. The key, however, is to come to the table with the right mindset and expectations. To do that, you should know what makes a negotiation winnable.

Negotiations are an integral part of the business world and a crucial part of the workday for many professionals. In fact, there are more than 1 million U.S. employees who negotiate on behalf of their employer each year, according to the Bureau of Labor Statistics. As such, many people have a general sense of what they want in a negotiation, but few know how to actually approach negotiations with the end goal in mind.

What makes a Negotiation Winnable?

The answer is simple: *Preparation.* If you have a good idea of your negotiating goals, you'll be able to focus your energy and prepare accordingly. Negotiating without a clear goal can lead to wasted time, money, and effort. To negotiate successfully, start with these four keys:

- **Know your goals** – Understand what you want to achieve, as well as the risks and costs of failure. Knowing your goals will help you focus your preparation and strategy.

- **Have a plan** – Develop an understanding of how you want to structure your negotiation – How do you want to deal with the other party? How should you present yourself? How do you want to approach the negotiation? What are the main issues? Do you want to play offense or defense? Do you want to win or do you just want to avoid losing?

- **Prepare to walk away** – You need to be prepared to walk away if the other party isn't willing to negotiate in good faith. If you are not willing to walk away, you will lose even if you have the best of intentions.

- **Communicate** – Effective communication is key to winning a negotiation. Use your body language and voice tone to convey the message that you are serious about reaching an agreement. Avoid speaking too quickly and don't speak too softly; both are indicators that you are not serious. Remember that you are dealing with a person and not just an object or a commodity.

- **Be flexible** – Flexibility is key to negotiating successfully. You can't expect the other party to change their position.

So; what are your negotiation goals? Below, we've listed a few of the most common goals for negotiating. Your goal as a business owner should be to grow your business. You should always keep this goal in mind. It's not as simple as knowing your opponent's position and then hammering them with it. Instead, it's about understanding the other person's needs, wants and expectations and coming to the table with a clear idea of how you can meet both of those goals. Negotiations are complex and unpredictable, so having the right mindset is key. One of the most important aspects of negotiation is being able to frame the issue in a manner that allows you to win. If you are at a disadvantage, then framing the issue in a way that makes the other side see your side as having the upper hand is essential.

Negotiations are a part of business life. Sometimes they are necessary and even fun, but at other times they can be stressful and draining.

Here are six tips for making a negotiation winnable.

1. **Set a win-win goal:** You may have already tried to achieve this goal in a previous negotiation and been unsuccessful, but if you really want to win, set a new one.

2. **Choose your side carefully:** You may want to choose your side because you want something specific (say, an offer), or because you feel obligated to take this path (for example, you don't want to rock the boat with a client). Either way, you need to understand why you're choosing this side.

3. **Don't make excuses:** If you don't have a reason for making a choice, you're giving up a chance to win.

4. **Negotiate in small steps:** If you've just met someone,

it can be tempting to throw out the first offer you think of. But this is a bad strategy because it may lead to a lot of time spent on small, unproductive concessions. It's better to start off with a simple, small request that can help you move closer to your goal. Then once you've agreed on this, you can ask for something more.

5. **Give yourself time:** Don't expect to get everything you want in one go. You'll get what you negotiate for, but you'll need to be patient.

6. **Be persistent:** Keep asking for things until you get them. If someone says no, don't be discouraged. Just ask again, with a little more detail and/or a slightly different approach.

10 Rules to Remember When Negotiating

The secret to effective negotiation is in having the confidence to ask for what you want. Whether you're dealing with a small business owner who needs to purchase a specific item, or with a large corporation that wants to offer you a position at a higher pay rate than what you currently earn, you need to show your value to the other party. Know your worth, and if the other party doesn't seem to care, ask yourself why. There could be an underlying issue that needs to be addressed before you can move forward.

This may seem like common sense, but in most cases people don't think about negotiating as a process. Asking for what you want means being clear about your value, knowing what's reasonable for your market, and being prepared to walk away from the table if necessary. When you know how to negotiate effectively, you can get more of what you want out of life. These negotiating rules are not a secret. The problem is that you hear these rules over and over and they seem to lose their effectiveness when repeated. But the truth is that if you break them down, they're actually easy to understand and easy to implement.

Here's a list of 10 rules for negotiating you need to remember.

Rule 1: Know your market: You must be able to clearly articulate the value you bring to the table. Don't let anyone tell you differently. If you want to go into business with someone, or even start a relationship, you need to know what you're buying. Your time, energy, and money are all commodities. You need to know what it's worth to the other person before you start negotiating. If you don't know what you want, then there's nothing to negotiate. You might as well just walk away.

Rule 2: Know what you want: Don't let others tell you that you can have something they think you should want. Don't get so caught up in wanting something that you lose sight of what you really want. The key is to figure out what it is you truly want. What would make you happy? What would you do if you didn't have to worry about making a living? Rule 3: Know what you need. You can't negotiate if you don't know what you need. If you don't know what you want, you won't know what you need. But if you do know what you need, you'll be able to say no to things you don't want.

Rule 3: Know what you deserve: Don't settle for less than you deserve. You need to get everything you can. If you want something that's not your right, you might as well just walk away. I don't think you're asking the wrong question. It is a perfectly legitimate question to ask why it is that we are here. The answer, however, is not that we are here because of some arbitrary plan or fate. We are here because of God, who made us in His own image. He loves us and created us for a purpose. I think this question is a good one. I think it's important to know why we're here. I think it's important to know what our purpose is. And I think it's important to know what we deserve.

Rule 4: Know when to say no: When you're going after something you don't really want, you need to learn to say no. Say no to the people who want you to do things you don't want to do. Say no to the requests that are not in your best interest. Learn to say no. It's okay. You'll get over it. It's a part of life. If you can learn to say no, you'll live a better life. *See also List of fictional newspaper reporters References Category:Fictional reporters Category:Fictional characters introduced in 2008Q*

Rule 5: Know Your Value and Understand How Your Market Values You: Asking for what you want is a numbers game. If you can't explain your value in dollars, you will not get what you want. You have to know how much your market values you. Then you can ask for what you want. For example, if you're working at a $15/hour wage, and you expect to be paid $20/hour, it's obvious that you're not worth $20/hour. The only way you can get what you want is to ask for more money or to negotiate to reduce your value. Otherwise, you'll end up with less than what you deserve. This rule applies to everyone. If you don't know your value, you won't get what you want.

Rule 6: Don't Talk About Money: There's no question that money is one of the most important things in life and we all have an opinion about how much it should be worth. However, when negotiating, don't even mention money or discuss your financial situation. This will give the other side the impression that they can take advantage of you, or worse yet, they'll try to play on your emotions.

Rule 7: Do Your Research: Before you go into any negotiation, do your research. Learn as much as you can about the other party before going in. Find out where they work, what they like, what they're looking for, and anything else that might help you win.

Rule 8: Always Be Prepared: When negotiating, be prepared. Bring a notepad with you, write down everything that you want to say and what you expect the other side to say. It's also good to write down questions that you have so that you don't forget to ask them during the negotiation.

Rule 9: Don't Get Too Personal: The last thing you want to do is get too personal during a negotiation. If the other side gets to know you, then they will be able to tell what you're really thinking. They will then be able to manipulate you, and it will be much more difficult to win in the long run. This will give the other side the impression that they can take advantage of you, or worse yet, they'll try to play on your emotions.

Rule 10: Set Your Boundaries: Don't give in to the other party's demands unless they are in line with your own expectations. You can't be happy if you're constantly compromising your standards.

Special Bonus

SPECIAL BONUS!

Want These 2 Bonus EBooks For Free?

Get FREE, Unlimited Access To These and All of Our New Books By Joining Our Community

CLICK HERE TO JOIN

Thank You!

Thank you for taking the time to check out my work - I hope you enjoy reading it as much as I enjoyed writing it! Authors wouldn't be anywhere without readers like you, so your support **REALLY** means a lot. I'm a firm believer that books don't need to be expensive or difficult to get hold of - so I want to encourage **EVERYONE** to enjoy the pleasure of books - and not just mine.

<u>I would be grateful if you could **WRITE ME A REVIEW** on the product detail page about how this book has helped you. Your review means a lot to me, as I would love to hear about your successes.</u>

Nothing makes me happier than knowing that my work has aided someone in achieving their goals and progressing in life; which would likewise motivate me to improve and serve you better, and also encourage other readers to get influenced positively by my work.

<u>Your feedback means so much to me, and I will never take it for granted.</u>

I'd love to hear from you if you have any recommendations

of your own, so please do get in touch if you've read anything awesome lately.

If you ever have any questions, you can get in touch at sam@samamoo.com.

I want you to enjoy your reading experience; your satisfaction is my number one priority. You are well appreciated for reading this book.

Thank you, have a wonderful day!

About The Author

Sam O.A is a writer and publisher focused on business growth, habits, decision making, and continuous improvement. He is the author of Sell Like Titans.

He teaches business owners on how to grow and run business at the same time, without getting stuck between the two worlds of growing and running business. He helps entrepreneurs build their dreams, by combining *concepts, ideas, and insights to make problem-solving easy.*

He has trained over four hundred successful business owners, and mentored over a hundred entrepreneurs excelling in digital and online business. Everything he does is fueled by his love for entrepreneurship, wealth development, diversity, and advancement.

Connect with us here:

Instagram: https://instagram.com/_amoosam

Facebook: https://fb.me/samamoo.official

Twitter: https://twitter.com/samamooofficial

LinkedIn: https://www.linkedin.com/company/samamoo

Email: sam@samamoo.com

Other Books

- How to be More in Tune with The Feelings of Your Customers
- Time Management For Busy People
- Sell Like titans

www.ingramcontent.com/pod-product-compliance
Lightning Source LLC
Chambersburg PA
CBHW072021070526
44583CB00015B/1575